Praise for *What Is Your WHAT?*

"Every once in a while a book comes along that stands out in its ability to really help people. If you are one of those people who feels unsatisfied with your work or still haven't figured out what you want to do when you grow up, read this book, do the brilliantly constructed exercises and watch your life transform."

—**Jack Canfield**
Cocreator of the *Chicken Soup for the Soul* series and
coauthor of *The Success Principles*

"This isn't a book as much as it is a road map. It takes you on a journey where you'll meet the most interesting character in the universe (Spoiler Alert: It's YOU). But the YOU that embarks upon this journey will not be the same YOU that reaches the horizon . . . in fact, *What Is Your WHAT?* will specifically guide you, step-by-step toward something most people never discover . . . and with this discovery you can, as Steve Jobs suggested, 'put a dent in the universe.' This book clearly puts the author, Steve Olsher, in the Who's Who of What's What."

—**Dan Hollings**
Marketing Strategist
www.danhollings.com
*(best known for his work with "The Secret," Zero
Cost Marketing Secrets, and Email Clockstar)*

"We are told the biggest regret shared by people in the last days of life is that they did not live an authentic life. Busy living out the expectations of others, they tried to be 'responsible' and 'practical,' but missed the one thing that would have made them great. In this timely book, Steve draws from the examples of people living their *WHAT* to give each of us a step-by-step process for living authentically. Prepare to become who you were born to be."

—**Dan Miller**
New York Times best-selling author of *48 Days
to the Work You Love*

"In every generation, there are a mere handful of books that truly stand out to people looking to get ahead in life in a positive and uplifting way. Steve Olsher's *What Is Your WHAT?* is in that elite field and needs to be read (make that devoured!) and applied today."

—**Ric Thompson**
Healthy Wealthy nWise

"I believe we are all created by God with a unique set of passions, talents, skills, abilities, personality, and presence that make us unique. That means you are the only one that can bring your unique value to the world! In *What Is Your WHAT?*, Steve Olsher helps you identify and move forward into what you were born to do. That fire burning inside you? It's calling you to impact the world. Do it!"

—**Joel Comm**
New York Times best-selling author
www.JoelComm.com

"I spent years figuring out what I was meant to do and it boiled down to a simple idea of helping others live their Full Potential. Steve has simplified the process and asks important questions that will help you go deeper in less time. If you're like me and tend to be overly analytical, this book will help you overcome perceived obstacles and take action. You don't choose your 'one thing,' it chooses you . . . and similarly, you don't choose this book . . . it chooses you!"

—**James Rick, "Mr. Full Potential"**
Founder of FullPotential.com

"Far too many struggle with defining who they are and what they were put here to do. In *What Is Your WHAT?* Steve Olsher shows you exactly how to tap into your natural wiring so you can monumentally impact not only those who share this lifetime with you, but also those of lifetimes to come."

—**Bill Renkosik (aka Bad Boy Bill)**
International DJ and Producer
www.badboybill.com

"If you're ready to learn a blueprint for discovering your true talents, skills, and abilities, then read and absorb the strategies in this book by Steve Olsher!"

—**James Malinchak**
Featured on ABCs Hit TV Show *Secret Millionaire*;
Coauthor, *Chicken Soup for the College Soul*;
Founder, www.BigMoneySpeaker.com

"Following the existential question of 'Why am I here?' that each of us strives to understand is the as-important 'What is my *WHAT*?' Avoid starting with the enigmatic 'Why,' and rather, seek your '*WHAT*.' When you discover it, you'll undoubtedly realize deeper meaning, fulfillment, and a sense of purpose unlike anything you've ever known!"

—**Mike Muhney**
Coinventor of ACT! Contact Management software;
CEO and Inventor of VIPorbit Mobile
Relationship Management software
www.MikeMuhney.com and www.vipOrbit.com

"Some people are just lucky . . . they immediately know who they are and what they were born to do. For us mere mortals, the process is typically a journey—one of trial and error. Identifying who you are and WHAT you were born to do can be daunting. With Steve Olsher's book, *What Is Your WHAT?*, you no longer have to go it alone. The answers you need are right here."

—**Bryan Toder, The No Fear Guy**
www.TheNoFearZone.com

"In *What Is Your WHAT?* Steve Olsher shows you how to move from being awake to being ALIVE. Seriously . . . life is short. Read this book, discover what you were born to do, share your gifts with the world, and get paid extraordinarily well for what you would gladly do for free."

—**Suzanne Evans**
www.SuzanneEvans.org

"If you've been frustrated with the direction of your life and there is a part of you that knows you are meant for something bigger, *What is Your WHAT?* is a must read! Why continue to try and figure things out on your own when Steve can show you the way?!"

—**Joe Amoia**
The Smarter Dating Guy;
Creator of Smarter Dating for Women
www.SmarterDatingForWomen.com

"Moving into our own unique focus is not a luxury, living authentically demands that we move onto our own path. Yes we get to fill in the blank! Moving to that which whispers to us, demands our attention and ultimately leverages our best is what we are designed to do and through these remarkable stories and exercises, Steve Olsher provides evidence on authentic living being the best measurement of success."

—**Deb Ingino**
Strength Leader
www.StrengthLeader.com

"*What is Your WHAT?* will make a positive difference in your life. If you've ever wondered, 'Why am I here and how can I turn my joy into my job?'—this book shows you how. Read it and reap."

—**Sam Horn**
Author of *POP!* and SerenDestiny®
www.SamHorn.com

"What Is Your WHAT? encourages you to hone in on the one trait every successful entrepreneur I have interviewed on my top-ranked business podcast EntrepreneurOnFire has . . . FOCUS: Follow One Course Until Success. We all have the ability to be AMAZING at one thing if we put our mind and heart to it. Podcasting is my *WHAT.* What is yours?"

—**John Lee Dumas**
www.EntrepreneurOnFire.com

"Steve Olsher has been helping people discover their *WHAT* for years. His powerful tools and technologies are only exceeded by his inspirational voice and from-the-heart encouragement and coaching. Steve has inspired me personally, and I know he will inspire you too."

—**Christopher Van Buren**
LaunchMoxie, Inc.
www.LaunchMoxie.com

"Identifying the ONE thing you were born to do and sharing this gift with the world is both your obligation and your birthright. *What Is Your WHAT?* not only teaches you precisely how to tap into your inherent blueprint but also to understand how you're uniquely wired to excel. I highly recommend reading it."

—**David Riklan**
Founder of www.SelfGrowth.com,
1 Self Improvement Website on the Internet

"Steve has created the ultimate guide on self-discovery and formulates a vortex of personal purpose and practical application. It's apparent that his *WHAT* was designed to ignite the fire in many souls to serve the world in whatever capacity they choose."

—**Erika Gilchrist, "The Unstoppable Woman"**
www.ErikaGilchrist.com

"You wish you knew how certain people became successful and could apply a process to your own life to get results. This book tells the story of successful people but more importantly teaches you how to duplicate their success by applying principles and strategies. Read it and watch your life change."

—**Andy Traub**
Author, *The Early To Rise Experience Series*
www.takepermission.com

"In a world full of fuzziness and confusion, this book is like a tiny grenade of clarity. Sharp, smart, and to the point, it's a perfect way to figure out your WHAT."

—**Jon Acuff**
New York Times best-selling author of *Start*
www.JonAcuff.com

"Stop passively going through life and start really living! *What is Your WHAT?* provides easy-to-implement solutions that will transform your life into one with great meaning and happiness."

—**Elizabeth Lombardo, PhD**
Best-selling author of *A Happy You: Your Ultimate Prescription for Happiness*
www.AHappyYou.com

"Steve Olsher has done a stellar job in reminding us of the key to really engaging with our life and work. A direct, engaging, and useful manual for connecting with our own unique signatures, and why that matters."

—**David Allen**
International best-selling author, *Getting Things Done: The Art of Stress-Free Productivity*
www.DavidCo.com

"Most people don't say 'YES' to what truly puts fire in their soul. Too often, they're living small and take misguided actions because they have yet to identify their *WHAT*—the ONE thing they were born to do. Until your *WHAT* becomes clear, you'll continually be led astray by distractions. Read this book, discover your *WHAT*, and say YES to life!"

—**Loral Langemeier**
The Millionaire Maker
www.LiveOutLoud.com

"Most people who ask themselves, 'What is my purpose in life?' go blank. Steve's book provides a definitive map to answer that question and most importantly shines a light on the final destination. *What Is Your WHAT?* takes you on a new journey of self-discovery and, ultimately, leads you to discover what you were born to do."

—**Steven Aitchison**
Author of *Change Your Thoughts*
www.stevenaitchison.co.uk/blog

"I'm a rabid fan of self-employment as the greatest vehicle for freedom in today's culture. After years of consulting with hundreds of people trying to go from traditional employment to 'free agency' and often running aground, I realized most failed business attempts come as a result of personal issues. Not understanding one's place in the world . . . the *WHAT* . . . is at the epicenter. Steve hooked me in his introduction through his personal story, fervor, and wisdom. This will be a foundational book in my business arsenal for helping my members."

—Kevin Miller
Founder of www.freeagentacademy.com

"Challenging, thought-provoking and insightful—a great exploration into becoming the you who you are meant to be."

—Randy Gage
Author of the *New York Times* best seller, *Risky Is the New Safe*

"Until you retrain the brain and transform your self-view, you'll continue to sabotage. Olsher helps you identify your best self and harness that power to fuel your breakthrough!"

—Lisa Jimenez M Ed
Best-selling author of *Conquer Fear!* and *Radical Transformation!*
www.Rx-Success.com

"Steve Olsher's concept and method for finding your *WHAT* is brilliant. We have an obligation to ourselves to pursue our passion and share our unique gifts with the world. This collection of stories from Steve's network of experts is sure to inspire and motivate readers to discover their *WHAT* and start living the life they were meant to live."

—Robin Jay
Award-winning Filmmaker,
www.TheKeyMovies.com

"*What Is Your WHAT?* guides you to achieve clarity and focus while empowering you to maximize your life production and quality. Read it and win."

—Dr. Bob Wright
Coauthor, *Beyond Time Management* and *Business with Purpose*

"If you're tired of wandering aimless in the world and have been searching for a solution to help you connect to your passion, *What is Your WHAT?* is a brilliant masterpiece that will transform your life and empower you to realize your highest potential."

—Robbie Tolk
Founder of Secrets to Healing
www.SecretsToHealing.com

WHAT IS YOUR *WHAT?*

STEVE OLSHER

WHAT IS YOUR *WHAT?*

DISCOVER THE
ONE AMAZING THING
YOU WERE **BORN TO DO**

WILEY

To the bold and fearless who pursue their WHAT with strategic abandon and have the courage to massively impact both those who share this lifetime with them and also those of generations to come.

The world is waiting for you.

CONTENTS

ACKNOWLEDGMENTS

There are many people who've supported me on my journey. My heartfelt thanks goes to the following:

- Lena, the love of my life, who makes the world a better place to be, always keeps me on point with her guidance, support, and compassion, and had the courage to pursue her *WHAT* at age 40 even though it meant starting completely over.
- My three sons, Bobby, Isaiah, and Xavier, for helping me to recognize that love truly knows no bounds.
- Mom, Al, Sylvia, Irv, Dad, and Barb (who created the visuals for *The Pinnacle Pyramid, The Vitality Curve,* and *The Circle of Four*), for helping to make me the man that I am.
- Elizabeth Nichols, for your incredible graphics and ability to create visual representations of my often difficult to decipher thoughts.
- Hy Bender, the world's best editor, for continuing to teach me the difference between writing and being a writer.
- Rania El-Sorrogy, for envisioning the modified Pinnacle Pyramid.
- Team Bold—Lori, Adam, Brittney, and Sean—for absolutely everything you do to empower others to discover and monetize their unique Gifts.

I love and appreciate each of you and could not have written this book without you.

You forever have my gratitude.

WHAT
IS YOUR
WHAT?

INTRODUCTION

I am only one,
But still I am one.
I cannot do everything,
But still I can do something;
And because I cannot do everything,
I will not refuse to do the something that I can do.
—Edward Everett Hale

Have you ever wondered why we so dearly love the story of Cinderella, the downtrodden servant who becomes a princess? Or the tale of Luke Skywalker, a humble farm boy who becomes the savior of the galaxy?

If you think deeply about their stories, you'll realize that while they undergo great transformations, they don't change from being one type of person to being an entirely different person.

Instead, they start out with their inherent greatness suppressed by difficult childhoods and buried by harsh circumstances. Over the course of their adventures, however, they learn to shed the shackles of their past and become their true selves—leaders, inspirational figures, and heroes.

The central message of these stories has great resonance for all of us. As we endure life's hardships, we tend to lose touch with our inner greatness. We start to make distasteful compromises, settle for less, and become people different from our deepest selves.

What Is Your WHAT? empowers you to follow the examples of Cinderella and Luke. If you diligently work through this book's exercises, you'll discover your true potential, become who you were born to be, and achieve profound fulfillment and success.

This will benefit not only you, but the lives of everyone you touch. Once you shed your skin and dump your baggage, you'll possess the magic to positively affect an incredible number of people.

Examples of this process go well beyond fairy tales. Consider the journeys of Mahatma Gandhi, Mother Teresa, and Dr. Martin Luther King Jr., three of the most revered and influential people of the past century.

None was born rich or powerful, but each tapped into a personal blueprint to access natural *Gifts*; determined the best way, or *Vehicle*, to make use of those Gifts; figured out who their primary audience was for those Gifts; and then moved Heaven and Earth to share those Gifts with the world.

In other words, they discovered their *WHAT*, pursued their *WHAT* with strategic abandon, and persevered until they provided the benefits of their *WHAT* to those who needed it most.

This is a path that's been followed since the beginning of mankind to achieve dramatic success. It's a model you can, and absolutely should, leverage.

Discovering your *WHAT* requires taking three steps:

1. Identifying your natural God-given Gifts.
2. Identifying the best Vehicle for sharing your Gifts with the world.
3. Identifying the specific audience who will benefit most from your Gifts.

After you've made these discoveries, you can maintain clear focus by articulating them in a summary that will serve as your life's guiding mantra.

If you have yet to identify your *WHAT*, don't worry; you will by the time you're done with this book. And in the meantime, you're far from alone.

The tragic truth is most people will reach their deathbeds without taking even one of the three steps to self-fulfillment; they will fail to recognize they were put on this planet to achieve something amazing.

A small number will manage two of the steps. And a very, very small percentage will accomplish all three.

This is in part why so many people are obsessed with celebrities who appear to be "living the dream." How else can we explain the tremendous popularity of shows about becoming successful in Hollywood, or why some people will spend hours in the rain just to catch a glimpse of a movie or TV star?

We're naturally attracted to those we believe are living their lives to the fullest: people who touch our souls, inspire us to take action, and are living their *WHAT*.

The good news is there's no privileged secret you must magically uncover in order to join the ranks of those "living the dream." All you have to do to achieve happiness and prosperity is discover your WHAT, work your tail off, and share your Gifts with the world.

It really is that simple. The world is waiting for you.

The Wisdom of Curly

There are numerous ways to describe your WHAT. One of my all-time favorites can be found in 1991's *City Slickers*.

In this movie, Mitch Robbins (played by Billy Crystal) takes a break from his busy Manhattan lifestyle to vacation at a dude ranch in the country in an effort to "find himself" and work his way out of a mid-life funk. During this journey, he meets Curly Washburn (played by Jack Palance), who represents everything Mitch is not: carefree, tough as nails, and—most importantly—centered.

I've seen thousands of movies in my life, but there are only a handful that really hit home. What most stuck in my mind from *City Slickers* was a scene that immediately seemed oddly profound, but I didn't take in its full meaning until years later.

It involves Curly and Mitch, each riding horseback, conversing about life. If you haven't seen the movie, try to imagine a tough, no-nonsense old cowboy wearing a black cowboy hat, red bandana around his neck, black riding gloves, and a lit cigarette hanging tenuously from the corner of his mouth. His voice sounds like it was passed down from Moses, and he talks with the confidence of a man who's seen and lived it all.

In comparison, Mitch is a small, unassuming city guy who's wearing a New York Mets baseball cap, and a shirt and khakis that might've come from L.L. Bean. The best way to describe the difference between them is this eloquent comment Curly makes to Mitch earlier in the movie: "I crap bigger than you."

In the scene that had the greatest impact on me, Curly says, "You city folk, you worry about a lot of shit."

Mitch replies, "Shit?! My wife basically told me she doesn't want me around."

Curly chuckles. "Is she a redhead?"

"I'm just saying—"

Curly interrupts. "How old are you . . . 38?"

"39."

"Yeah. You all come here at about the same age with the same problems. Spend about 50 weeks a year getting knots in your rope, and then you think two weeks out here will untie them for you. None of you get it. Do you know what the secret of life is?"

"No, what?"

Curly smiles and holds up one finger: "This."

"Your finger?"

Still holding up one finger, Curly says, "One thing. Just one thing. You stick to that and everything else don't mean shit."

Mitch holds up his own finger. "That's great. But what's the one thing?"

Curly says, "That's what you've got to figure out . . . ." And then he rides away.

Curly calls it your "One Thing." I call it your WHAT. It doesn't matter what you call it. You just need to figure out what it is.

Your Two Choices

You now have two choices:

1. Complete this book in its entirety, identify your WHAT, wear your WHAT on your sleeve, and share your unique Gifts with the world, or

2. Accept that your current vocation *is* your WHAT, live it as best you can, and quit your complaining.

You may be thinking there's just no way the latter is true. For example, if you work with numbers, you might say to yourself, "Spend the next 50 years with clients running spreadsheets, filing tax returns, or planning retirement portfolios? Absolutely not!"

But if you grew up with a flair for math and solving complex equations resonates to your core, then being an accountant or financial planner could be what you are truly compelled to do.

That said, there have been skilled number crunchers who started as part-time bookkeepers and ended up creating financial sector-related endeavors that earned millions.

You don't have to consciously take the three steps to your WHAT to realize your path. Some lucky people naturally find it right away, while others make subtle adjustments over the course of years until they're where they need to be. Still others make an abrupt 180° turn at some point and start a whole new career.

An example of the latter is Dr. Joe Amoia of Emerson, New Jersey. Joe spent tens of thousands of dollars and more than 15 years of his life becoming a licensed chiropractor, opening his own practice, and developing hundreds of loyal patients. If you'd asked him eight years ago whether he'd be dropping his practice and changing careers, he would've laughed at you.

But, today, Joe is the *Smarter Dating Guy*—a dating and relationship strategist who coaches single women on how to find love.

Why would a successful doctor willingly walk away from what he'd worked so hard to attain? What empowered him to start over from scratch?

He discovered the one thing he was born to do. And once he identified his *WHAT*, virtually everything else became trivial.

Your WHAT *isn't something you choose. Your WHAT has chosen you.*

In contrast, the vast majority of people never find their path . . . mostly because they refuse to recognize it exists.

Even when clients are interested enough to attend my workshops, there are always some who resist the concept. They ask:

"How is it possible that someone has just one thing she overwhelmingly loves to do?"

"What if I don't have a *WHAT*?"

"Why should I spend my time figuring out what my *WHAT* is? My life is just fine."

It saddens me when people resist discovering who they are and the Gifts they possess. It saddens me even more, however, that some of our world's best minds and most passionate souls have identified their *WHAT* but are stuck in situations that deprive them of the opportunity to fully achieve their greatness.

If you're reading this from the comfort of an easy chair, a park bench on a beautiful day, or your favorite coffeehouse, count your blessings. Recognize that anything and everything you desire can be yours—because you possess the freedom to pursue your destiny.

Put away all excuses. Be grateful for the opportunities available to you and, most importantly, prepare yourself for a life-altering journey.

A Little About Me

I grew up in Evanston, Illinois, a child of modest beginnings. My parents divorced when I was seven. My brother, sister, and I lived with my mom, who did her best to raise us on a limited income.

I started working at age 10. I took on all kinds of odd jobs—shoveling snow, raking leaves, mowing lawns. If it paid anything, I grabbed it.

In high school I had a 4.0 GPA. I'm not talking Grade Point Average, but Girls Per Attempt. In other words, for every 10 girls I asked out, I averaged four dates.

That actually wasn't bad for a short wannabe player with a frizzy mullet and a gold hoop earring (see Figure I.1). During high school I waited tables, pumped gas, fixed cars, played drums, stocked shelves, worked in restaurants, and even sold speakers out of the back of a van.

Figure I.1   Steve in High School

During my freshman year of college, I began to DJ, and eventually became good enough to spin in the clubs throughout Illinois. This led to my sharing the stage with some of the biggest DJs in the late 1980s and early 1990s, including Bad Boy Bill and Julian Jumpin' Perez.

At age 20, I opened The Funky Pickle! on the main drag in Carbondale, Illinois, just off the campus of Southern Illinois University. The Pickle was a unique concept—a no-alcohol nightclub in the middle of Carbondale's alcohol-suffused nightlife. At first glance, it seemed like a huge mistake, but I had a plan.

I knew the local teenagers had very few options for entertainment. So from 8:00 p.m. to 11:30 p.m., we catered to those under the age of 18. At 11:30 p.m. we closed, cleaned the place up, reopened at midnight and catered to those 18 and over . . . often until 6:00 a.m.

By city ordinance, bars that served alcohol had to close at 1:30 a.m. Given that we didn't have a liquor license, we could stay open all night long—and we had plenty of customers who appreciated that. Ultimately I had a falling out with my business partner, but with this first success, my entrepreneurial fire was fully ablaze.

I've since gone on to build multiple million-dollar businesses in various fields, including Liquor by Wire (starting as a catalog company, then launching on CompuServe's Electronic Mall in 1993, and becoming one of the first ecommerce websites in 1995); Liquor.com (as cofounder and chairman); and Bold Development (a real estate development company that focuses on adaptive reuse) and I have applied creative approaches to each endeavor.

Not all of my ventures have proven fruitful and I've experienced monumental ups and downs. I've gone through financial ruin, divorce, and battles with depression. But I've also fallen back in love, been blessed with three wonderful children, and built very successful companies.

I've been married to my wife Lena since 1997 and have three incredible sons. Nothing teaches you more about life than love. Love requires patience, kindness, and selflessness—traits that don't always come naturally to me. I work at it every day. And while I often make mistakes, the look of disappointment in the eyes of someone I love always brings me back to center.

Since August 2000, I've trained in Brazilian Jiu-Jitsu under one of its true grandmasters—Carlson Gracie Jr.—and the late Carlson Gracie Sr.

Carlson Gracie Jr. is a legend in the sport, having won 10 Brazilian Jiu-Jitsu championships, and is a member of the family that put Brazilian Jiu-Jitsu on the international map. If you're unfamiliar with Jiu-Jitsu, it's a ground-fighting technique in which the objective is to force your opponent to surrender. This subtle persuasion takes place as a result of chokes or limb manipulation (think broken arms, legs, ankles, elbows, etc.). Being choked to the point of unconsciousness and having limbs twisted in directions you never thought humanly possible has resulted in my learning humility and respect in the most painful of ways.

In early 2009, everything shifted. My stepfather, who'd raised me since I was 10, was home in bed dying. The illness he'd fought against for years was finally winning. As we sat together, I held his hand. Though he could no longer verbally express himself, I believe he spoke to me through our physical connection.

A vision of *my* funeral flashed before my eyes. As I was being lowered into the earth in the dark, damp casket, I could hear the words spoken graveside: "Here lies Steve Olsher. He dedicated his life to chasing the almighty dollar." That's all that was said.

It was a huge wake-up call that slammed me with the force of a kick to the head. I began to think about what accomplishments I could look back on at the end of my life that would make me feel proud. Interestingly, none of them involved making money.

I'd always had a nagging feeling I was meant to do something extraordinary. The funeral vision made clear that the path I'd forged was leading me away from my natural talents. I was being told to change course. I faced what I now call a *YāNo* (pronounced Yay-No) moment. It's a pivotal moment of truth that can lead you in either of two directions:

1. Away from honoring who you truly are, or
2. To the path that best aligns with your core being, and allows the *You* of tomorrow to look back and give thanks to the *You* of today.

I've since learned there's a significant difference between living well and living for the sake of making money.

Don't get me wrong; each of us is entitled to make a phenomenal living. You shouldn't have to apologize for charging what you're worth or resign yourself to life as a starving artist simply because you're compelled to create art. If a top athlete can earn millions for hitting a ball with a stick, why shouldn't a top artist sell paintings, books, or screenplays for millions if that's what the market will bear? And if money isn't your bag, give it away and support your favorite charity.

Ultimately, we're all obligated by our common bond of humanity to pursue not only what brings us financial success, but also what can make a positive impact on our community, our country, and our world. In the years since beginning my transition, I've learned to embrace and develop my intuitive Gift for helping people discover their WHAT. Following this path has led me to

- Costarring in the groundbreaking film *The Keeper of the Keys* with Jack Canfield, John Gray, and Marci Shimoff
- Founding and running *The Reinvention Workshop,* which many participants have described as creating the pivotal event in their lives (TheReinvention Workshop.com)
- Founding and hosting *Reinvention Radio* (ReinventionRadio.com), "the show dedicated to creating empowered leaders driven to make a monumental difference"
- Writing the Amazon.com bestseller and USA Book News Self-Help Book of the Year, *Journey to You: A Step-by-Step Guide to Becoming Who You Were Born to Be* (JourneyToYou.com)
- Writing the Business Technology Book of the Year, *Internet Prophets: The World's Leading Experts Reveal How to Profit Online* (InternetProphets.com)
- Founding and hosting Internet Prophets LIVE! the premier Internet, mobile, and marketing workshop, where the world's best gather to share their knowledge and help participants use that information to change their lives (InternetProphetsLive.com)
- Leading The Circle of 10 (CircleOf10.com), a private, 12-month coaching program that empowers entrepreneurs to realize the income they deserve and lifestyle they desire
- Appearing on the ABC and FOX television networks and more than 300 radio shows, including national programs hosted by Lou Dobbs, Jim Bohannon, and Mancow Muller

Perhaps most fulfilling, I now have the opportunity to speak to people of all ages and see the light in their eyes as they envision creating a life filled with fulfillment, success, and happiness.

I'm not recounting the highlights of my life to boast, but to explain my motivation for writing this book. It's these life experiences that formed this book's bluntly honest, cut-to-the-chase perspectives about personal growth.

Please Take the Shortcut

I wrote *What Is Your WHAT?* because I want you to celebrate the Gifts that are uniquely yours, share your special talents with the world, and become who you were born to be.

I've developed and refined the proprietary exercises, theories, and principles you'll find in these pages over the past 25 years. They're crafted from my own (often painful) hands-on experience. I've made the mistakes and suffered the inevitable results so you don't have to.

I'm a steadfast believer that we should learn from the trials and tribulations of others. I've been fortunate to benefit from the guidance of incredible teachers. I hope that you'll allow me to mentor you.

My unique methodology blends ancient wisdom (e.g., from Buddha, Lao Tzu, and The Bible) with revolutionary lessons from modern gurus (e.g., Jack Welch, David Allen, and Larry Winget). These teachings, combined with my unique exercises and singular approach to realizing permanent, positive change, form a proven system for ultimate achievement in business and life.

To aid you in your process of discovery, you'll find scattered throughout the book stories and completed WHAT equations from members of my private coaching program The Circle of 10 (CircleOf10.com) and graduates of The Reinvention Workshop (TheReinventionWorkshop.com) who have transformed their lives using this system. You'll also find completed WHAT equations from people whose work you may know, such as Jack Canfield, Chris Brogan, Marci Shimoff, Guy Kawasaki, and Mari Smith, who I sat down with to discuss the key steps along their path of discovering and sharing their WHAT with the world.

As I've mentioned, your WHAT is comprised of three interdependent elements. To maintain a clear focus on your WHAT, I recommend crafting a concise guiding statement that summarizes those elements. Figure I.2 shows an example of a completed WHAT equation.

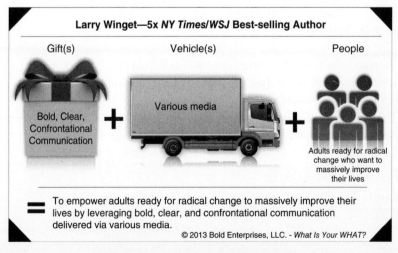

Figure I.2 Sample WHAT Equation

This book will teach you how to compose your own *WHAT* equation. It'll also introduce you to powerful shortcuts you can use immediately to move towards the life you deserve.

Of course, you have to do more than just read; you must work through all of this book's exercises and make full use of its tools. In the words of Jim Rohn, the author and motivational speaker who helped launch the careers of such personal development icons as Tony Robbins and Mark Victor Hansen, "You can't hire someone else to do your push-ups for you."

By the time you're done with this book, you'll have a clear understanding of your life's purpose; and be fired up about, and highly focused on, achieving it. And if you then do the work to bring your *WHAT* to fruition, you'll enjoy immense emotional and monetary rewards.

How This Book Is Organized

What Is Your WHAT? is organized into three parts.

Part I empowers you to *Establish the Foundation*, and demonstrates how *The Four Stages of Learning* impacts who you are and why you do what you do. You'll learn how to set deep anchors into your soul that keep you on your path (as opposed to being a windsock, continually blown off course by external forces). You'll tap into your formidable inner strength and learn to handle certain areas of your life with such mastery that to the rest of the world you'll appear magical.

Part II teaches you how to realize *Permanent, Positive Change* and introduces you to *The Seven Life-Altering Principles (The S.L.A.P.)*. Each principle provides powerful life strategies and helps you establish clear guidelines for living with conviction and purpose. You'll explore the pitfalls that trip up far too many on the path to prominence and learn the most effective strategies for attaining your goals and objectives.

Part III guides you to *Become Who You Were Born to Be* by teaching you how to answer the key question: What Is Your *WHAT*? Identifying your *WHAT*, and allowing it to guide you to your pre-sent future, will lead you to a freedom beyond anything you've experienced. You'll also learn what to do after discovering your *WHAT*, and how to attain a clear understanding of who you are, what you were born to accomplish, and how to realize your inherent greatness.

What You Will Achieve

Completing *What Is Your WHAT?* will empower you to

- Shed the shackles of your past and reconnect with who you really are.
- Leverage your natural talents, honing in on the key areas for which you're wired to excel.

- Uncover and eliminate barriers you've unconsciously created.

- Realize fundamental change at the deepest level of your being—change that will become inseparable from your thoughts and actions.

- Identify your *WHAT* and establish a plan of action for sharing your *WHAT* with the world.

- Identify your life's purpose, your goals, and the factors that motivate and inspire you.

- Achieve peace and prosperity.

I firmly believe The Destination *Is* the Road and The *Journey* Is the Destination. *What Is Your WHAT?* is a quest for the most precious of destinations: your true self.

Let's begin your journey.

Establish
the Foundation

CHAPTER

1

Introduction to the Four Stages of Learning

Most people live, whether physically, intellectually or morally, in a very restricted circle of their potential being. They make use of a very small portion of their possible consciousness, and of their soul's resources in general—much like a man who, out of his whole bodily organism, should get into a habit of using and moving only his little finger. Great emergencies and crises show us how much greater our vital resources are than we had supposed.

—William James

What if someone you love more than anyone else in the world is dying of a rare disease and only has six months to live? And, what if you Google this disease and learn of a miracle antidote owned by a rain forest shaman (who's also a capitalist) that costs $1 million and you only have $1,000 to your name?

How hard would you bust your butt to make that $1 million? How quickly could you turn the impossible into the definite? Like a finely tuned, high-performance sports car, you operate with multiple gears. Seldom, however, are you faced with crises or emergencies that require you to maximize your potential and fully leverage your abilities that, in turn, creates dynamic results.

Have you ever heard a story about a terrified mother lifting an impossibly heavy object to free her child from harm's way? Or a father who fights off a wild animal with his bare hands to protect his family? While, hopefully, you'll never be faced with one of these situations, the fact remains that your life is governed by the self-imposed limitations you've established. Such limitations run the gamut from repeating self-defeating phrases such as "I could never do that" to maintaining destructive ways of being, such as staying at a job you loathe because you've convinced yourself that you have no other options.

> *Ultimately, the further you can stretch these limitations,*
> *the more fulfilled you'll be.*

As William James observed, most people use a very small portion of their possible consciousness and of their body's resources in general. You hold the power to kick your life into overdrive. However, you also hold the power to continue coasting. As evidenced by the aforementioned examples, if one has the power to create extraordinary results when pushed to the brink, is it then possible for this to be a repeatable action that can be called upon as needed? Couldn't extraordinary performance become the go-to way of being as opposed to the other way around?

Close your eyes and establish a clear vision of the person you love more than anyone else. Now, remember they have just six months to live and you can be their hero by securing the funds necessary to purchase the antidote. In my presentations and workshops, I ask attendees to consider this scenario and raise their hands if they believe they could deliver the $1 million by hook or by crook, doing whatever it took, within six months to save this person's life. Consistently, more than 90 percent will indicate that, yes, they could make this happen.

Could you? If so, and you're willing to operate at maximum speed to save someone you love, what speed are you willing to travel to save yourself?

Creating Your Foundation

In order to discover your WHAT and share the one amazing thing you were born to do with the world, you first need to understand who you are. This is essential for manifesting long-term, sustainable change that continually supports the realization of your goals and objectives.

Part I of this book helps you create this change by identifying the cravings of your being and the restricting forces that prevent you from living the life you deserve and desire. Few people reach their potential because they operate like a windsock—letting chance dictate their lives and moving in whatever direction the whims of others takes them. The process of personal transformation is too often similar to the "new car high" many experience. For the first few months, the love is deep. Each week, the car is washed, waxed, and vacuumed. After a period of time, however, the love fades, and what was once a prized possession becomes just another car.

I don't want this to happen for you. Therefore, to remain focused and inspired, you'll need to set deep anchors into your soul and establish an unyielding foundation upon which to build a new, more powerful you. This will prevent you from being "enlightened" for a brief period of time and then returning to old habits.

Picture a beautiful glass and steel skyscraper built upon an unstable base. While passers-by may admire the impressive structure that reaches for the stars, a weak infrastructure below the surface will eventually send the whole building toppling to the ground. My objective is to help you construct an unshakable footing that will support the person you'll be once you've completed this book. Without resolute grounding, you, like the poorly constructed skyscraper, will find yourself unstable in your approach to life, easily swayed by those trying to blow you off path, and continually thwarted in your desire to achieve meaningful satisfaction and contentment.

To create an extraordinary life, follow what I call the *Path to Freedom*. This requires you to:

- Become aware of strengths and self-imposed limitations.
- Make a conscious choice about what to do with these strengths and limitations.
- Improve upon, maintain, modify, or eliminate them.

One of the most effective tools for obtaining such understanding and creating the necessary blank slate for reinvention is the *Four Stages of Learning*. While very powerful, the Four Stages are a bit dry. Please grab a glass of water and bear with me as I take you through it. I promise you'll reach the other side with a compelling new perspective on your life and the strength required to stay clear, focused, and fired up about becoming who you were born to be.

The Four Stages of Learning

The discovery that there are four distinct stages of learning comes from Thomas Gordon, who in the 1970s developed the Conscious Competence Learning Stages

Model. It was first published in his *Teacher Effectiveness Training Instructor Guide* and is widely used in academia and business to this day.

Behind this bland academic title lies the key to understanding why you're able to excel in certain aspects of your life and lag in others. The four stages are:

1. **Unconscious Incompetence:** Not knowing what your strengths or problems are or how to identify them.

2. **Conscious Incompetence:** Having the ability to identify strengths or problems but not the desire or knowledge to improve upon or correct them.

3. **Conscious Competence:** Having the proficiency to achieve your desired results but needing to be consciously focused on your process as you perform the actions required.

4. **Unconscious Competence:** Having the proficiency to achieve your desired results without having to think about your process (a.k.a. "The Zone").

Figure 1.1 details Gordon's model. It illustrates how the process of learning begins at the stage of Unconscious Incompetence—exemplified by low resistance, little time expended, and a high degree of incompetence—and flows to Unconscious Competence—exemplified by low resistance and a high degree of competence with little time expended to attain one's desired results.

Ultimately, your goal is to attain the stage of Unconscious Competence in as many areas of your life as possible. Many correlate this stage with having achieved "mastery." The world applauds and generously compensates those who have become a master of their craft. While pursuing mastery of additional skills should be your ongoing objective, mastering even one skill can result in significant spiritual and psychological benefit for both you and those you touch.

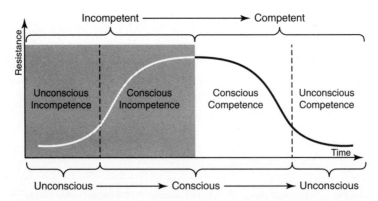

Figure 1.1   The Conscious Competence Learning Stages Model

You have the ability to inspire the world. Let's look at Gordon's *Four Stages* model and how its revolutionary approach to understanding how we learn is an extraordinary tool you can leverage to create the results you want and shed the habits you don't.

Stage One: Unconscious Incompetence

In this stage of learning, the following characteristics are present:

- You're not aware of strengths or problems.
- You're not aware that you lack a course of action to benefit from strengths or address problems.
- You might deny the relevance of strengths or problems and/or usefulness of the strengths or missing skills.
- You must become conscious of strengths or problems as well as your incompetence to improve upon or address them before the process of attaining mental or physical proficiency can begin.

Put simply, in this stage of learning you're not aware of your strengths or problems, or your inability to address them. Life in the stage of Unconscious Incompetence is exemplified by a "What's wrong with the rest of the world?" attitude. Within this unaware state, it's everyone else who doesn't "get it" and you experience frustration due to your inability to recognize personal shortcomings or strengths.

You must be ruthless with yourself to identify where you live within the state of Unconscious Incompetence, and in the next two chapters, I'll show you how. Until you're willing to reclaim control, your life will run on autopilot, and your reactions to the world will continue to be what is most familiar and most comfortable. This is a destructive pattern that eliminates the possibility for growth. And if you're not growing, you're dying.

To become aware of issues that you don't realize control your quality of life, commit to exploring who you are and why you do what you do. This will take more than simply reading. It requires completing the exercises in this book. The most effective way to approach each exercise is with an open mind and without distractions. Be brutally honest and write down exactly what comes to mind. Try not to let fear or self-sabotaging thoughts interfere with the process.

Taking on your reinvention from a place of denial, or with the concern that others are going to read through your notes and get mad at you for what you've written, is counterproductive. This is your private journal. Protect it as such.

Treat each exercise as if your life depends on the quality
of your results. It does.

While doing so may sometimes be difficult, it's the only way to extinguish the components of who you are that aren't serving you well. Otherwise, the "old you" will come back with a vengeance and overthrow everything you've learned. This is not an option. The next chapter, "The Vortex of Vulnerability," begins your exploration of Stage One—Unconscious Incompetence—and presents one of the most challenging exercises in this entire book.

It asks you to dig deep to identify hidden elements of your personality and underlying drivers that largely control your life. Once you're able to recognize these mischievous sprites, you'll hold the power to either permanently eradicate them from your thoughts or continue to allow them to come along for the ride. It's time to disengage the cruise control.

Introduction to The Four Stages of Learning—Takeaways

- The further you can stretch your self-imposed limitations, the more fulfilled you'll be.
- Most people operate like a windsock—blown about by the whims of others and never realizing their potential.
- Set deep anchors into your soul and establish an unyielding foundation upon which to build a new, more powerful you.
- Follow the path to freedom:
  - Become aware of strengths and self-imposed limitations.
  - Make a conscious choice about what to do with these strengths and limitations.
  - Improve upon, maintain, modify, or eliminate them.
- The Four Stages of Learning is a powerful tool you can leverage to create the results you want and shed the habits you don't.
- The world applauds and generously compensates those who have become a master of their craft.
- Stage One is Unconscious Incompetence. In this stage, you lack awareness of your strengths and problems, as well as your inability to improve upon or address them.
- You must be ruthless with yourself to identify where you live within the state of Unconscious Incompetence.
- Treat each exercise as if your life depends on the quality of your results. It does.

WHAT IS YOUR *WHAT?*
Case Study #1: Marci Shimoff

Marci Shimoff is a #1 *NY Times* best-selling author, celebrated transformational leader, and one of the nation's leading experts on happiness, success, and unconditional love. A featured teacher in *The Secret*, she is the author of *Love for No Reason*, *Happy for No Reason*, and six best-selling titles in the *Chicken Soup for the Soul* series, including *Chicken Soup for the Woman's Soul* and *Chicken Soup for the Mother's Soul*.

President and cofounder of the Esteem Group, she delivers keynote addresses and seminars on self-esteem, self-empowerment, and peak performance to corporations, professional and non-profit organizations, and women's associations. A top-rated trainer for Fortune 500 companies, Marci inspires with her breakthrough methods for achieving personal fulfillment and professional success.

Getting to this point, however, required significant trial and tribulation. At 13, her life was forever altered when she attended a Zig Ziglar seminar. From that point forward, she was driven to pursue a career in speaking and, after earning her MBA from UCLA, began as a corporate trainer teaching Stress Management and Communication Skills. Though she generally enjoyed her work, she lacked genuine fulfillment.

It wasn't until 1995, while on a seven-day silent meditation retreat, that the platform she would leverage to share her gifts en masse would become clear. On the fourth day, she envisioned creating *Chicken Soup for the Woman's Soul*. Three days later, when her silence could be broken, she contacted her mentor Jack Canfield who absolutely loved the idea. 18 months later the book was released and the rest is history, or in this case, (her) story…

Marci is a *Shifter* and her *WHAT* is defined below. Visit HappyForNoReason.com for more information.

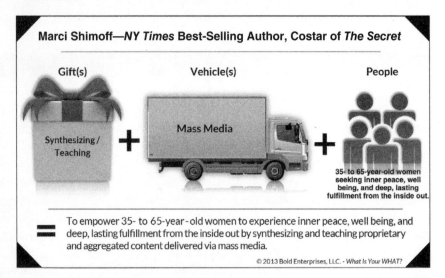

Marci Shimoff—*NY Times* Best-Selling Author, Costar of *The Secret*

Gift(s)	Vehicle(s)	People

Synthesizing / Teaching

Mass Media

35- to 65-year-old women seeking inner peace, well being, and deep, lasting fulfillment from the inside out.

= To empower 35- to 65-year-old women to experience inner peace, well being, and deep, lasting fulfillment from the inside out by synthesizing and teaching proprietary and aggregated content delivered via mass media.

© 2013 Bold Enterprises, LLC. - *What Is Your WHAT?*

CHAPTER

2

The Vortex of Vulnerability

Knowing others is intelligence; knowing yourself is true wisdom.
Mastering others is strength; mastering yourself is true power.

—Lao Tzu

There's an old adage that says, "Better the devil you know than the devil you don't."

It's true that we typically fear the unknown much more than the familiar. But positioning yourself to look what you *don't* know in the eye—and refusing to back down—will empower you to achieve breakthrough results.

The Vortex of Vulnerability will help cultivate this strength. It's composed of a three-step process. Each step will help you gain clarity as to who you are and why you do what you do. When combined, the steps will help you move forward with conviction and purpose, and reveal aspects of your life you aren't consciously aware of but that have a profound impact on your behavior.

Let's begin.

Step One

Identify three recent times in your life when you absolutely lost it.

Losing it varies for different people. It might mean yelling at someone at the top of your lungs, sending a nasty email, or not returning someone's phone call.

The specific way in which you lose it isn't important for this exercise. What matters is that you identify the times when you've lost control and resorted to your most primal, or natural, way of being. Take the time to replay these moments in your mind with as much detail as possible.

Think about what set you off. What led to the exact moment when you could no longer think straight? Now identify your physiological state at that time. How did your body feel when you lost it? Did your face turn red? Did you cry? Was your breathing short and did your chest feel tight? Were your shoulders hunched forward? Did your head feel heavy? Did you want to scream?

Here's how Mary B. of Louisville, Kentucky, a participant in The Reinvention Workshop, described her memory of losing it: "I screamed at my son for spilling his bowl of cereal. When I saw the cereal all over the floor, it hit. My body felt tight. I could feel my blood pressure rising. My face scrunched up. I wanted to punch something. I just couldn't help my reaction."

Write your three "losing it" moments here:

1. _____
2. _____
3. _____

Step Two

Identify three moments in your life that had major life-altering ramifications.

Such moments may be either positive or negative. The idea is to gain an understanding of the key moments in your life that helped shape you into the person you are today. Examples of life-altering moments include:

- The day your father sat you down and told you he was leaving home
- The time when you were in the fifth grade and blew a really loud fart in the middle of silent reading time and everyone thought you were hilarious from then on
- The day you graduated from college
- The first, and only, time you got into a fistfight

Think about how you felt when these moments transpired. If it was a negative moment, were you scared? Did you cry? Did you vow to never again perform the activity that led to that moment? If it was a positive moment, did your self-esteem fly through the roof? Did you get a huge smile on your face? Did your body feel light as if you were floating? Did you later try to replicate that feeling as often as possible?

Now try to figure out how you embedded these moments into your psyche. In other words, how did you turn them into character traits that became a permanent part of how you identify yourself and how other people identify you?

Here's how Todd S. of Arlington Heights, Illinois, another Reinvention Workshop participant, described his turning point:

I remember the exact moment my father told us he was leaving our family. I cried, and felt scared and alone. I internalized the moment to mean that if my father—who supposedly loved me—could abandon me, then I must have become unlovable.

From that point on, no matter how much love anyone gave me, I was always left starving for more. I would expect to disappoint people and lead them to abandon me, sabotaging good relationships before anything bad could happen. I wanted people to see me as tough so they knew to not mess with me or try to take advantage of me.

Write your three life-altering moments here:

1. _____

2. _____

3. _____

Step Three

Identify how you believe the world sees you versus how you'd ideally like to be seen.

This is known as a "disconnect," and there's often a huge difference between these two frames of mind. While you may believe your actions reflect your conscious desires, this is seldom the case. For example, you may want to be loved and appreciated by those within your circle, but your circle may see you as difficult due to your consistent complaining or obnoxious ways of interacting. Take a moment to give yourself a reality check to determine if the way you want to be perceived by the people around you reflects how they actually see you.

Next, identify your state of mind when there's a clash between how you'd like to be seen and how you're actually seen. When your friends view you as being difficult, do you argue and, consequently, validate their point of view? Do you write people off when they don't "get you"? How do you feel when you act in a certain way to achieve a particular goal and fail?

Here's how James T. from Miami, Florida, an online Workshop participant, described his disconnect:

I want the world to see that I'm a kind and generous person. However, people seldom care to spend time with me or talk to me on the phone. They accuse me of being self-centered and uncaring. This really hurts because I know I'm a good person. I go out of my way to help others, yet no one seems to appreciate this. Therefore, I just stop trying. When people do call me after two or three weeks of not hearing from them, I don't respond very nicely. I think I'm trying to punish them for not seeing all of the good I have to offer. I internalize this cycle to mean I must be unlikable, and therefore I act in an unlikable manner.

Write your three disconnects here:

1. _____

2. _____

3. _____

Review of Step One

In Step One, you were asked to identify *three recent times in your life when you absolutely lost it*. The purpose is to help you understand which events throw you off balance, causing you to lose perspective. Being able to recognize what drives you to the edge of disaster is the first step toward reclaiming your life.

Look back at the times you identified. Chances are they happened in response to situations in which you felt out of control. Identifying similarities among situations that make you feel out of control will enable you to become keenly aware of when you're likely to lose it. Start to recognize these as *danger zones* that can create great harm.

It may take you a while to know what sets you off. Once you do, though, you'll stop reacting in an *automatic* way—that is, the way you've responded until now—and instead behave in a manner that's appropriate to each specific situation.

For example, if you lose it when your child spills something, venting may give you temporary relief but at the terrible cost of damaging your overall goal of a close, loving relationship with your child. As another example, if you lose it when someone cuts you off in traffic, your natural response to chase him down and curse him out could result in your getting the tar beaten out of you . . . or even being shot.

Think of your life as a series of scenes that adds up to an epic film. Now think about which characters within your movie play an instrumental role in the outcome of your story. Your movie has lead actors, supporting actors, extras, and so on. Some of these characters have an ongoing presence in your film. Others appear for just a few seconds.

You must become highly focused on any person with whom you are about to wage war. If it's someone of great importance to you, look for alternatives to conflict. Conversely, if it's someone of little importance to you, then why bother? Consider likely outcomes, be selective about which mountains you're willing to die on, and be sure to weigh the punishment against the crime.

Get to the Root of the Problem

Look at your list again and try to identify the cause for your behavior. I want you to become familiar with the circumstances that surround your losing it so you can be prepared to control your response when faced with similar situations.

If you can raise your awareness of places where potential trouble lurks, you can begin planning alternate routes of travel. Try to understand where your difficulties in these particular aspects of your life originated, and think about what drives you to the point of wanting to hurt that which, oftentimes, is most dear to you.

Here are some examples of triggers that may have resonance for you:

- Losing your mind when someone is slow to understand you
- Deflecting a compliment
- Becoming infuriated by a political conversation
- Being in a bad mood for days because you failed to complete a certain task

John C. from Chicago, a participant in The Reinvention Workshop, used to get terribly upset when he'd have to repeat himself. He eventually came to realize that he associated this behavior with feeling unimportant and "small." As a child he was left out of adult conversations because his father often said, "Children should be seen and not heard." Ever since—even into adulthood—he unconsciously feared that what he had to say wasn't worth hearing. Anyone not hearing him for the first time triggered this insecurity.

Understanding this allowed John to adjust his attitude and accept such situations at face value. Now, instead of becoming upset when he has to repeat himself, he simply moves closer to the person with whom he's speaking, says his words again, and continues the conversation. End of problem.

Becoming aware of your inner demons will empower you to use rational thought and find the appropriate course of action for uncomfortable situations. When this happens, you'll shift from punishing people innocent of the past "crime" that's upsetting you to experiencing unfiltered reality. By mastering the skill of seeing situations clearly and reacting appropriately within the context of the situation, you'll join the ranks of a very select group of peers.

Review of Step Two

In Step Two, you were asked to identify *three moments in your life you would describe as having unequivocal, life-altering ramifications*. The goal is to shed light on the events you most closely associate with your sense of self, and to understand how these events affect you.

Look at your list. Some of the moments you've identified may be traumatic, such as a car accident or a divorce. Other life-altering moments may be positive, such as graduating, getting married, or having a child. Either way, these incidents make up a critical part of who you are.

Consider your behavior in relation to the events you've identified.

Your personality, and the ways in which you interact with the world, are directly related to how you've internalized your life-altering moments.

Let's look at a couple of examples that illustrate your power to create the life you desire.

Jackie L. of Indianapolis was physically and emotionally abused as a child. As an adult, she is both untrusting and scared of intimacy. Though this is an understandable response, others who endured similar abuse have adopted the opposite approach and become warm, loving, and giving people.

Raul R. from Encinitas, California, was convicted of a violent crime when he was 18 years old and served 10 years in prison. After his release, he decided that he never wanted to be locked up again. He now devotes his life to helping others avoid similar mistakes.

Far too many who have been convicted end up as repeat offenders or walk around full of resentment, blaming the world for their problems. You have many different paths to choose from after experiencing a life-altering moment. This is the time to ask yourself whether the path you've selected is serving you well.

Your Life, Your Choice

People have argued for centuries over whether we're more influenced by nature or nurture—nature being who you are as a result of your genes and nurture being who you are as a result of your upbringing.

Bottom line: For you, it's irrelevant. You hold complete control over the choices you make now—and the wisdom of those choices will determine the quality of your life.

No matter what happened in the past, you can commit to thinking and acting in ways that benefit you from this point on. You can make that decision right now and make it again for every moment that follows.

Recognize that you're not the person you have defined yourself to be, nor are you merely the culmination of a series of events. The character traits you've developed by internalizing your life-altering moments are always within your power to maintain, alter, or fully release.

Don't use the past as an excuse for current behavior that serves you poorly. Take responsibility for who you are right now.

In Chapter 10, "Retrain Your Brain," I'll introduce you to methods for approaching life with a blank slate. For now, simply decide that who you are, and how you behave from this moment forward, won't be driven by your past.

Review of Step Three

In Step Three, you were asked to *identify three examples of how you believe the world sees you versus how you'd ideally like to be seen.* The purpose is to help you understand how dramatically you're affected by the disconnect between these two realities.

Look at your list. If you were brutally honest, what you've written may alert you to lies you've been living. Our intentions are often very different from our actions, and this can create serious problems.

For example, a manager I know considers himself a good boss by checking on the work of his employees several times a day. But his staff considers him a control freak, and most of them are planning to leave as soon as possible for a job where they will be treated like responsible adults.

As another example, a father of one of my son's classmates considers himself devoted to his children, but he frequently breaks promises to them when an activity they've planned interferes with his job. Should this pattern continue, over time his children will lose their trust in him and start to believe that he loves his work more than he loves them.

The disconnect can be buried so deep in the state of Unconscious Incompetence that the person is unable to recognize that a problem even exists, let alone that his behavior is the cause of it.

Reconnecting the Disconnects

Disconnected states will inevitably lead to frustration and unhappiness. To identify these states in your life, explore the areas where you experience dissatisfaction, and then probe for the causes.

For example, if you're having internal dialogues filled with negativity, or if you're constantly putting out fires, the odds are good that a disconnect is at the root of the problem. When you recognize this happening, think hard about the situation or interaction you're facing and whether your behavior truly represents your intentions.

To establish a platform of strength and stability, you must be willing to cure that which ails you, even if you don't know what it is.

If you can move each disconnect out of your state of Unconscious Incompetence and into your state of consciousness, and then make deliberate choices to align your internal dialogue and actions with your intentions, you'll take a powerful step towards improving your life.

"Bonus" Step Four

CAUTION: Take this step only if you can handle constructive criticism from the people closest to you . . . and are willing to risk the consequences.

If you're having difficulty identifying your disconnects, one of the most effective ways to uncover them is to conduct no-holds-barred discussions with those closest to you about how they see you versus how you see yourself.

This step isn't for everyone. It can lead to long-term hurt feelings and can even destroy fulfilling relationships.

That said, if you have the steely disposition to handle blunt honesty, this is the process to follow:

1. Create a list of questions for which you'd like feedback. Here are some examples to consider:

   - I believe I'm a good friend. Do I act that way?
   - I feel I'm always there when people need me. How do you feel about that?
   - I think I usually have nice things to say about people. Have you found that I actually tend to bad-mouth others?
   - People like spending time with me. Would you say this is accurate?
   - Based on my history and how I interact with others, I believe I'm a smart person who makes wise decisions. Do you agree?
   - I feel good about where I work and what I do. How often do I complain to you about my job?

   Take the time to put together a thoughtful list of questions so you can make the most of this opportunity.

2. Start with one person in your closest circle. Do *not* do this with a group! (You'll feel defensive and attacked working with just one friend or family member, let alone a small mob.) Let this person know you want her honest, constructive feedback. Make it clear that you won't become angry, no matter what is said, and you won't let this conversation affect the relationship. (Obviously, if you can't fully commit to these promises, do *not* take this on. Simply proceed to the next section.) Be prepared to take notes—or, better yet, bring along a digital recorder that's tiny enough to be ignored but powerful enough to preserve hours of conversation. Your loved one has been storing up these comments for years and will have plenty to say.

3. Be prepared for a litany of observations that may leave you feeling awful about yourself. Don't get angry or defensive—after all, you asked for this. However, it's okay to request clarification on comments you don't fully understand and to ask your loved one to expand on items that really hit home.

4. When the session is over, offer heartfelt thanks to the person you chose. Make it clear that you truly appreciate her honesty.

5. Internally, disassociate the feedback you received from the person who gave it to you. If the information is accurate, where it came from is unimportant. Simply focus on the discoveries you've made and how you can benefit from them.

6. Repeat the process with other members of your closest circle—but always with one person at a time.

This experience will be harsh. However, nothing will give you more valuable insight into how the world sees you than honest feedback from loved ones. Once you have the information, use it to repair the disconnects you've discovered. At that point, you'll be able to move your life forward with better clarity and focus.

The Vortex of Vulnerability: Aligning the Pieces

To complete the Vortex of Vulnerability, examine the items you've identified and look carefully for correlations.

For example, in Step One you might have noted one of the times when you lost it as happening in the presence of your father; in Step Two one of your life-altering moments might have occurred when your father abandoned you and your mom; and in Step Three you may have written that you see yourself as a sweet, kind, loving father, but your kids never call you. This sort of pattern makes clear that your childhood relationship with your father has had a major impact on your adult behavior.

On the lines that follow, write down all of the commonalities and patterns you notice from reviewing your answers to the three (or four) steps of this exercise. Please take your time on this final step; it's vital to understanding what's buried in your past that's working to your detriment. Focus on repeated themes, such as *family* or *work*, and write down whatever reveals itself to you.

_____

_____

_____

_____

To foster meaningful, permanent change, you must be willing to accept things that are hard to bear.

In this final step of your review, the negative emotional drivers that lead toward much of your unhappiness will float to the surface. While this can be painful, do *not* deny what's in front of you. If you combine your new understanding with courage and make beneficial choices, you'll be able to reinvent who you are.

If the commonalities and patterns aren't evident, don't panic. This exercise is designed to begin creating awareness. By learning to recognize the moments when you experience discontent, anger, or frustration, you'll start to identify your self-defeating catalysts. You can then take appropriate action.

For now, simply honor yourself for committing to this process of discovery. By doing so, you've embarked on a life-changing journey that will free you from the aspects of your life that have held you hostage without your consent . . . and worse, without your knowledge.

On to Greener Pastures

I recognize that the Vortex of Vulnerability can be difficult and may have brought some dirt to the surface. So let's take advantage of that dirt by planting flowers.

The next chapter, "The Vortex of Invincibility," will open your eyes to areas of your life where your soul truly soars.

The Vortex of Vulnerability—Takeaways

- Look for areas in your life where you tend to lose it, feel out of control, experience frustration, and/or become unhappy. These are danger zones that are likely to have significant impact on you.

- Become aware of your inner demons. This will empower you to use rational thought and find the appropriate course of action in uncomfortable situations.

- Identify where potential trouble lurks so you can plan alternate routes.

- Shift from punishing people innocent of some past "crime" that's upsetting you to experiencing unfiltered reality.

- Your personality, and the ways in which you interact with the world, are directly related to how you've internalized your life-altering moments.

- You hold complete control over the choices you make. The wisdom of those choices determines the quality of your life.

- Don't use the past as an excuse for current behavior that serves you poorly.

- Align your intentions with your actions.

- Strive to eliminate disconnects. If you feel it'll help, seek feedback from others to identify your disconnects.

- Perception is reality. Give yourself a reality check and be clear on how you're perceived.

WHAT IS YOUR *WHAT?*
Case Study #2: Rick Calvert

Rick Calvert is the CEO and Cofounder of New Media Expo, one of the largest gatherings of new media content creators in the world. His company, which was born from the simple idea of creating a venue for bloggers to congregate, has grown to include TBEX, the Travel & Blog Exchange, and the Small Business Summit.

An aspiring guitarist since the age of five, Rick began his professional career at a southern California music store in the hope of meeting other musicians. After just two weeks, he established his position as the store's top salesman. The owner (interestingly enough, a distant relative named Jerry Olsher) quickly recognized his potential and sent him to receive formal sales training. After several years, he shifted to the B2B market, eventually landing a national sales manager position with Gatorz Sunglasses. Here, Rick was tasked with setting up, driving traffic to, and manning Gatorz's booth at the Motorcycle Dealer Tradeshow. He thrived in this environment, feeding off the adrenaline of the crowd, thus marking the beginning of his love for tradeshows.

In 2005 as the Internet hit its stride, Rick launched a political blog. While searching for a tradeshow he could attend to gather with, and learn from, established bloggers his search came up empty. Consulting fellow content providers and potential tradeshow partners for validation, Rick began putting the pieces together to create an event that fulfilled *his* needs. Within less than two years, Blog World launched with over 1,500 attendees.

Today, Rick's events attract tens of thousands of attendees annually and he has positioned himself at the epicenter of three ever-evolving industries. Rick is a *Reinventor* and his *WHAT* is defined below. Visit BlogWorld.com for more information.

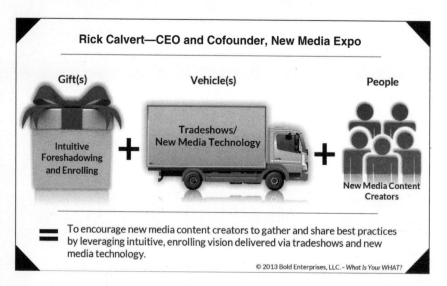

Rick Calvert—CEO and Cofounder, New Media Expo

Gift(s)

Intuitive Foreshadowing and Enrolling

+

Vehicle(s)

Tradeshows/ New Media Technology

+

People

New Media Content Creators

= To encourage new media content creators to gather and share best practices by leveraging intuitive, enrolling vision delivered via tradeshows and new media technology.

© 2013 Bold Enterprises, LLC. - *What Is Your WHAT?*

The Vortex of Invincibility

Be who you are and say what you feel, because those who mind don't matter and those who matter don't mind.

—Theodor Seuss Geisel

C hris Rock has said, "Life ain't short. Life is long!" If you aren't clear about what inspires you and moves you towards becoming your true self, life will be long, tedious, and disappointing.

The key to freeing your soul and encouraging it to soar is to recognize areas of your life where you excel. Once this happens, you'll begin to withhold power from the activities, people, and interactions that dare to clip your wings, and concentrate on what brings you the most joy.

The Vortex of Invincibility empowers you to make these discoveries. Each of its three steps (four if you choose to take on the Bonus) will reveal important aspects about you and allow you to hone in on your natural strengths. When combined, the steps will help you identify who you truly are and where you should focus your energy.

This chapter continues your exploration of Stage One—Unconscious Incompetence—and begins your journey toward becoming who you were born to be.

Let's get started.

Step One

Identify three positive moments in your life when time absolutely flew by.

At various times in your life, you've experienced this incredible feeling of lightness. It's as if the world melts away and nothing remains but you and your soul. Some have experienced this feeling when chatting with a loved one. Some feel this profound sense of stillness when meditating. Some feel it when participating in sports. Others tap into it when playing with their children.

When time simply flies by, you have achieved emotional nirvana. You simply are and have zero conscious thought.

Please take a few moments to identify three positive moments when you've achieved this all-too-rare state of peace.

Think about the circumstances involved. Where were you? Who were you with? What activity were you engaged in? Did this happen before or after another specific event?

Now identify your physiological state at that time. How did your body feel when you entered that zone? Did you feel light? Did you smile? Was your breathing full and did you feel completely relaxed? Try to remember as best you can how you felt in the exact moment when time stood still.

Here's how Rick G. of Naperville, Illinois, a Reinvention Workshop participant, described his time-standing-still memory:

> I remember the first time I went skydiving. All of my friends were nervous wrecks, but I was incredibly excited. My adrenaline was pumping like crazy. I was literally nowhere to be found. My friends said they tried talking to me, but I wouldn't answer. I was completely engulfed in the moment. As I stepped out the door of the plane, I experienced a sense of freedom unlike anything I had ever known. For what seemed like an eternity, the world was mine. I had never been in such an amazing state of peace.

Please write your three time-standing-still moments in the space that follows:

1. _____

2. _____

3. _____

Step Two

Identify the three people you most admire and the character traits they display.

Over the course of your life, you've encountered an enormous number of people. From friends and family you see often, to TV stars, spiritual leaders, and business icons you've never met, thousands have crossed your path. But only a select few leave an indelible mark. There's no denying that you're naturally drawn to some and repulsed by others.

While many inspire with their accomplishments or generosity, certain people simply "fit" better with who you are. This is not an illusion. Some say this feeling stems from encountering a kindred spirit. Others suggest it's from sharing a similar type of childhood. What matters is heeding the inherent truth of this connection.

Please take a few moments to identify the three people you most admire and the character traits they display. They can be living or dead, and people you know well or know only by name. Focus on the specific aspects of their personalities that ring true. Think about why each person makes your list. Why do they outshine the rest? What draws you to them?

Is it how they make you feel when you're in their company? Is it what others say about them, or their dedication to honing their craft? Is it the legacy they left behind, or the impact they had on the world? Be clear on the rationale behind your choices, and use adjectives to describe them—such as honest, determined, spiritual, compassionate, vulnerable, daring, intelligent.

This is how Carol V. of Los Angeles, an online Workshop participant, described one of the people on her list:

> One of my most-admired people is my grandfather. My earliest childhood memories include him and me playing sports, watching TV, or going out to eat. But what I most admired about him was his honesty. You could always count on him to deliver the truth. It was never presented in a way that inflicted pain. He was a master at that. No matter who it was, he was always able to tell them the truth and do so in a way that made them closer. He was one of those rare people who excelled in both his personal and business life. Looking back, I'm confident that his success was due to his incredible ability to communicate effectively. He just made everyone comfortable.

Please list the three people you most admire and their character traits here:

1. _____

2. _____

3. _____

Step Three

Identify three accomplishments or times when you've been proud of yourself.

Small victories win the war; within these victories hide the secrets to understanding where you're compelled to soar. By examining moments of excellence, you can extrapolate key indicators that define when you're operating in a manner that's congruent with who you truly are.

From winning awards and completing difficult assignments, to getting the companion of your dreams or hitting the game-winning shot, there were times in your life when you've succeeded brilliantly. Conversely, there were other times when you failed miserably. This is not a coincidence. Your DNA is programmed to excel in a very specific manner. To fight this is an effort in futility.

As an example, imagine Quentin Tarantino directing *Steel Magnolias*. While he certainly could have done the job, some characters would probably have ended up losing limbs, resulting in a different kind of story from what the writers and producers originally had in mind. The same holds true for you.

If you're a square peg, trying to jam yourself into a round hole will only result in pain.

Identifying moments of accomplishment or times when you've been proud of yourself will help you develop a clear sense of your personal "sweet spots." These moments reflect circumstances when everything aligns perfectly, and you're able to achieve astounding results with relatively little hardship. These moments may include being recognized for your contributions, rewarded for your abilities, trying something new and completing the task at hand, or feeling amazing because you participated in a particularly gratifying activity, such as helping someone in need.

Try to identify why you were compelled to succeed. Was it because of the person you were working with? Were you trying to impress a peer, coach, or mentor? Did someone say you could, or—often equally powerful—that you couldn't, accomplish your stated goal? Or was it because you were engaged in an activity that came as naturally to you as breathing?

Mark A. from Buffalo Grove, Illinois, a Reinvention Workshop participant, described this time when he was proud of himself:

> I remember when I was about 15, me and my family worked in a soup kitchen that our church arranged. We were there for over 10 hours. It was Thanksgiving, and there were many, many people who came to enjoy a nice hot meal. I was very tired at the end of the day, but I specifically recall feeling very proud of myself for taking the time to be there and help others. Obviously, we didn't get paid. That absolutely didn't matter. It just felt really good to be there and share the holiday with so many wonderful people.

Please list your three accomplishments or times when you've been proud of yourself and the reasons you believe you were able to succeed:

1. _____

2. _____

3. _____

Review of Step One

In Step One, you were asked to identify *three positive moments in your life when time absolutely flew by*. The purpose is to help you understand when you feel most at peace. Acknowledging these remarkable moments enables you to take a milestone step toward reliving this way of being as often as possible. By becoming aware of what makes you feel invincible, you can begin to understand where you'll find true fulfillment.

You may recall Step One of The Vortex of Vulnerability asked you to consider when you're likely to "lose it" and plan routes away from such situations. In contrast, Step One of The Vortex of Invincibility encourages you to steer your life *towards* the people, interactions, or activities that bring you the most joy.

Robin Davis of Los Angeles is a gifted singer who performs professionally. When she sings, life couldn't be sweeter. The stage is her home, and she often works gratis because there's no place she'd rather be.

Where do you feel most comfortable? Even if you didn't get paid a cent, what activities would you enthusiastically pursue?

Look back at the moments you identified, and examine what it is about them that you find gratifying. Is it that you're able to engage in the activity without fear or judgment? That you feel appreciated, listened to, or loved? That you achieve a state of mind where you can fully focus without interference from outside thoughts? That you're able to complete what you started? Whatever the reasons may be, embrace them. They are integral to what makes you tick.

Try to recognize commonalities in these moments and begin focusing on ways of being that require zero conscious effort, yet create an indisputable sense of comfort.

> **Too often, we concentrate on everything that's wrong instead of everything that's right.**

It may take you a while to embrace these aspects of who you are. But by prioritizing what's most natural for you and pushing what's not to the side, you'll have discovered one of the fundamental keys to living a rewarding life.

Once you have that combination in hand, you can use it to unlock the mystery of making time fly.

Review of Step Two

In Step Two, you were asked to identify *three people you most admire and the character traits they display*. The objective is to gain an understanding of who captures your interest and the motivation behind your attraction. This exercise functions like a mirror for the inner you, providing an honest reflection of who you inherently are. What you admire in others *directly reflects* what you most desire for yourself and provides insights about who you are. It's therefore very important to be completely honest when exploring why each person made your list.

For instance, if Microsoft founder Bill Gates is one of the people you named, what is it about him that you respect? Is it his business success, vision, willingness to take risks, philanthropic efforts, or notoriety?

If your sister is on your list, what is it about her you appreciate? Is it her openness, ability to communicate well, passion for life, or ability to love and forgive?

Try to pinpoint the characteristics that stand out. By identifying what you admire in others, you open the door to understanding how you're hard-wired to succeed. The odds are good that you, too, would excel if you focused on these particular areas of your life.

For example, if one of the people on your list is your mother and you admire her *tenacity*, *compassion*, and *ability to persevere*, the chances are good that, whether you demonstrate it regularly or it's suppressed deep within you, you also are *tenacious*, *compassionate*, and a person who *perseveres* no matter the circumstances.

Similarly, if you admire your coworker's *calm*, *creativity*, and *high-degree of integrity*, it's likely that you also possess these inherent traits.

Machiavelli said, "A prudent man should always follow in the footsteps of great men and imitate those who have been outstanding." This fifteenth-century politician's advice remains true to this day. Kobe Bryant, All-Star guard of the Los Angeles Lakers, has been compared to Michael Jordan, former guard of the Chicago Bulls, both for how he plays and how he communicates with the press and fans. Despite his achievements, Bryant's replication of Jordan's mannerisms, competitive spirit, and manner of speech is often criticized.

Given that Jordan has been consistently voted as the best basketball player of all time and led the Bulls to six NBA Championships, Kobe should have no shame for emulating him.

Imitation isn't merely the sincerest form of flattery. Replicating the actions and embodying the character traits of those you admire is a flat-out brilliant strategy.

To further understand this concept, consider those you deplore. What is it about them that makes your skin crawl? Is it their selfishness, cruelty, lack of integrity, or allegiance to something that goes against everything you stand for? By examining what you loathe in others and reversing those character traits, you'll find what most aligns with your personal aspirations.

The map that leads to your destiny is within you. Your job is to learn to read it and follow it.

Circle of Four

As you embark on your journey of discovering your *WHAT* and becoming who you were born to be, consider those with whom you choose to travel. A component of your success is establishing a *Circle of Four* that not only encourages you to reach your full potential but also accurately reflects who you want to become.

Your Circle of Four is made up of the four people you consider cornerstones. It includes both those you admire—such as a mentor who you seldom see but have access to—and those dearest to you, such as your best friend or closest family member. The sum of these four people directly reflects your life.

For example, the median net worth of your Circle of Four is likely to be very close to yours. If two in your Circle are broke and two have just enough to scrape by, the odds are good you're concerned about where your next meal is coming from. If your Circle of Four includes three people who consistently complain about their careers and one who is living their *WHAT*, it's likely you want better for yourself but aren't busting your butt to get there.

Be wary of those whose goals and objectives don't closely mirror or exceed yours. (See Figure 3.1.) While it may be comfortable to surround yourself with familiar faces, they must support your mission or their weight is going to drag you down. While it's a hard thing to do, it might be necessary to cut the rope if they

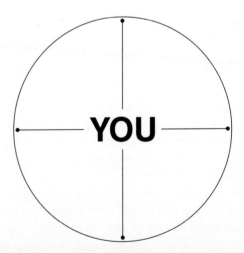

Figure 3.1   Be Fully Aware of Who You Surround Yourself With

hold back your efforts to soar. Take a few moments to review your current Circle. Be honest about what you see.

To flourish, you need accountability partners who both inspire and encourage you. Be conscious of the power your Circle holds. With the right people in your Circle, anything can happen. With the wrong people, nothing will. Choose wisely.

Review of Step Three

In Step Three, you were asked to *identify three accomplishments or times when you've been proud of yourself.* The purpose is to focus on moments when everything clicked and explore why you succeeded. Since childhood, you've proven over and over that you possess the ability to succeed. Whether it's walking, feeding yourself, or driving, when you've put your mind to it you've created your desired results.

The triumphs on your list represent natural talents. Accepting these Gifts as fundamental pieces of who you are will help you achieve long-term satisfaction.

Also understand your motivation to excel. Why do you believe you were able to perform in these particular areas? Were you inspired by a certain teacher? Did you have a coach who brought out the best in you? Were you determined to be recognized? Did you simply feel compelled to complete the task at hand? Try to recall your state of mind. There was something that ignited the flame. Take the time to uncover what it was.

Jack W. from Lake Geneva, Wisconsin, a personal friend, had been a C student for most of his life. In college, however, he earned an A in every economics class he took. While he felt he worked just as hard in other classes, he couldn't achieve the same results. Jack recognized his innate attraction to the subject, and he leveraged that Gift into becoming an economics professor at a well-respected Midwestern university.

The more you concentrate on the areas of your life that spur your soul and breed victory, the happier you'll be.

"Bonus" Step Four

If identifying your strengths is difficult, consult those closest to you. Those who care about you will support your personal development.

You may recall that Step Four of The Vortex of Vulnerability risks long-term hurt feelings and even the destruction of fulfilling relationships. In contrast, Step Four of The Vortex of Invincibility can create stronger personal bonds as you enroll others in your transformative process.

This is how I recommend you proceed to ask those who know you best for their opinions:

1. Create a list of questions. Here are some examples to consider:
   - What do you feel are my natural talents?
   - When have you seen me at my best?
   - Are there particular people I gravitate towards?
   - If you had to use one word to describe me in a positive manner, what would it be?
   - Are there certain activities at which I excel?
   - When do I seem most at peace?
   - What do others say they like about me?

   Take the time to put together a thoughtful list of questions so you can make the most of this opportunity.
2. Start with one person in your closest circle. Let this person know you want his or her honest feedback.
3. Be prepared to take notes—or better yet, bring along a digital recorder that's tiny enough to be ignored but powerful enough to preserve hours of conversation. Your loved one will have plenty to say.
4. Request clarification on comments you don't fully understand. Be sure to ask your loved one to expand upon items that really hit home.
5. When the session is over, offer heartfelt thanks. Express your love, and make clear you truly appreciate her honesty.
6. Focus on the discoveries you've made and how you can benefit from them.
7. Repeat the process with other members of your closest circle—but always with one person at a time.

Each meeting should be light, fun, and inspiring. Remember, you want to focus on the areas of your life where you excel. Once you have the information, use it to pursue what comes most naturally to you, and move your life forward with vigor and dedication.

The Vortex of Invincibility: Assembling the Puzzle

To complete The Vortex of Invincibility, examine the items you've identified, and look carefully for patterns.

For example, in Step One you might have identified a moment when time stood still as happening when you played sports. In Step Two, you might have chosen to admire Wayne Gretzky, arguably the best hockey player of all time. And in Step Three, maybe one of the accomplishments you listed was helping your high school sports team win the state championship. This sort of pattern makes clear that sports is an area of your life where you feel comfortable.

Write down all of the commonalities you notice from reviewing your answers to the three (or four) steps in this chapter. Focus on repetitive themes such as *family, sports, friendship, career*. Take your time, allowing yourself to uncover as much as possible.

_____

_____

_____

In this final step of review, the positive emotional drivers that lead to most of your fulfillment will float to the surface. Don't deny what you uncover. To effect meaningful, permanent change, you must be willing to accept how you're structured to thrive. If you then couple that understanding with supportive choices, you'll have the ability to reinvent your life.

If the commonalities and patterns aren't evident, don't panic. This exercise is designed to begin creating awareness. By diligently pursuing where you're most likely to experience peace, elation, and an undeniable sense of stillness, you'll expose your natural talents. This inevitably leads to focusing on activities and interactions where your soul soars.

The Completion of Stage One

This concludes your exploration of the first stage of learning—Unconscious Incompetence. The following chapter introduces you to the next three stages—Conscious Incompetence, Conscious Competence, and Unconscious Competence.

Get ready for liftoff!

The Vortex of Invincibility—Takeaways

- Recognize the areas of your life where your soul is wired to soar.
- Direct your life toward the people, interactions, and activities that bring you the most joy.
- Hone in on your natural strengths.
- Identify when you typically achieve emotional nirvana.
- Figure out why you're naturally drawn to some people and repulsed by others.
- Replicate the actions and embody the character traits of those you admire.
- Understand your personal victories to determine the areas where you'll flourish.
- Accept your Gifts as fundamental parts of who you are.
- Consider who's in your Circle of Four, and proactively choose to make required changes.
- Recognize your strengths. If necessary, recruit family and friends to help.
- The more you concentrate on areas of your life that breed victory, the happier you'll be.

WHAT IS YOUR *WHAT?*
Case Study #3: Larry Winget

Larry Winget is 'The Pitbull of Personal Development®' and 'The World's Only Irritational Speaker®.' A 5x *New York Times/Wall Street Journal* best-selling author of thought-provoking books including *Shut Up, Stop Whining & Get A Life*, star of the PBS special, *Success Is Your Own Fault*, frequent media guest, member of the International Speakers Hall of Fame who has spoken to nearly 400 of the Fortune 500 companies, and former host of A&E's *Big Spender*, few have such an impressive track record of success.

Yet, things weren't always this way. After an early career in sales, several successful entrepreneurial endeavors, speaking hundreds of times in formulaic, suit and tie manner, and publishing numerous books with (as he readily admits) uninspiring titles such as *The Simple Way to Success* and *Money Is Easy*, Larry hit the proverbial wall. Declaring he hated everything about his life including himself, he packed his bags and walked away from his family, friends, and career.

While gathering his thoughts beneath the red rocks of Sedona, Arizona he reconnected with his *WHAT* and chose to honor whom he inherently is—a brash, irreverent, bold, and honest communicator. He immediately called his wife to ask if she'd take him back (she said "*yes*") and his agent to announce his revelation.

Within months, he completely revitalized his life, dramatically shifted his approach to business, and fully embraced his Oklahoma roots by taking the stage (and subsequent book covers) in blue jeans, custom cowboy apparel, and colorful handmade boots. His unapologetic, no-holds-barred style has helped make Larry one of the most recognizable, highly paid, and polarizing speakers, authors, and commentators on the circuit today.

Larry is a *Shifter* and his *WHAT* is defined below. Visit LarryWinget.com for more information.

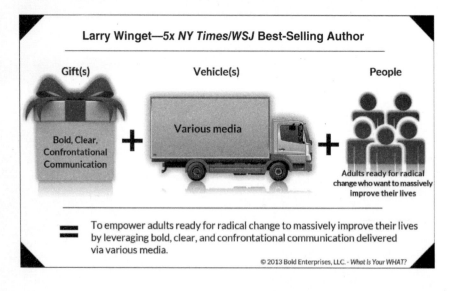

Larry Winget—5x *NY Times/WSJ* Best-Selling Author

Gift(s)	Vehicle(s)	People
Bold, Clear, Confrontational Communication	Various media	Adults ready for radical change who want to massively improve their lives

To empower adults ready for radical change to massively improve their lives by leveraging bold, clear, and confrontational communication delivered via various media.

© 2013 Bold Enterprises, LLC. - *What Is Your WHAT?*

CHAPTER
4

The Next Stages
of Learning

A sensible man will remember that the eyes may be confused in two ways: by a change from light to darkness, or from darkness to light. And he will recognize that the same thing happens to the soul.

—Plato

The next stage of the Four Stages of Learning is *Conscious Incompetence*. It has the following characteristics:

- You're aware of your strengths and problems.
- You're able to gauge the extent of your abilities and deficiencies, and the level of skills needed to maximize the former and modify or eliminate the latter.
- You commit to improve upon those skills so you can move to Conscious Competence.

Before entering into the state of Conscious Incompetence, you were living in the dark. Things simply happened and you didn't know why.

In this second stage of learning, your eyes are wide open and you can make informed choices. More specifically, you're aware of your strengths and problems, as well as your current deficiency in dealing with them.

As a result, you can make a conscious choice to either

- Take the necessary steps to gain competence in your core areas and reap the benefits, or
- Not try to gain the competence because you don't perceive the potential benefits outweighing the cost in time and energy.

Either way, you can say "I am in control of my life." You're now in a state of awareness.

Bringing to Light the Choices You Make

The following exercise will shed light on how this stage of learning affects you.

Please take a few minutes to write about three facets of your life where you possess some knowledge or ability to a *limited* extent, but are comfortable with the level of expertise you have. Also describe how you feel about owning your "incompetence" in this area.

Judy Y. from Ft. Lauderdale, Florida, an online Reinvention Workshop participant, wrote in response to this exercise:

I know I don't speak German fluently. I speak enough of the language to get by, but my abilities are limited. I'm perfectly okay with this because I don't have any business or social need to use the language.

1. _____
2. _____
3. _____

Now identify three of your relationships that are mediocre in quality, yet you've chosen to maintain them in their current form. Also indicate how you feel about continuing these relationships at this level.

Here are two examples from Jennifer K. of San Jose, California:

My brother and I haven't spoken for years. Part of me would like to have a relationship with him, but whenever we see each other we fight, so it's really not worth it.

My friend Louise and I aren't close anymore. It upsets me that neither of us commits the time to get together more frequently. I'd like to talk with her about this and see if we can rekindle our friendship.

1. _____
2. _____
3. _____

This exercise is designed to help you recognize the power you hold to improve upon strengths and modify or eliminate problems. The quality of your life depends largely upon your ability to recognize what you can and can't control. Problems falling within your state of Conscious Incompetence are fully yours to own and manage.

Stage Three: Conscious Competence

The third stage in the Four Stages of Learning is *Conscious Competence*. It has the following characteristics:

- You have the skills to effectively leverage strengths and address problems.
- You can demonstrate strengths and handle problems without assistance.
- You have to concentrate when demonstrating strengths and solving problems, as your abilities are not yet second nature.
- You can demonstrate strengths and problem-solving abilities, but you haven't mastered them well enough to do a great job of teaching your process to someone else.

In this stage of learning, you have *concentrated skill*. You can achieve your desired results because you have the ability to perform as needed. Living at this level is not your ultimate goal, though. Leveraging strengths and solving problems in the state of Conscious Competence too often requires expending a substantial amount of thought and effort, leaving you tired and, in all likelihood, unsatisfied.

To understand why, think about how a professional golfer swings a club. The swing is often compact, seeming to take little effort; and yet the ball scorches past 300 yards. An amateur can swing the club too, but has to put a lot of thought and effort into it. Further, no matter how much effort is expended, the ball won't travel beyond 240 yards.

To an untrained eye, the two swings may look similar. However, the novice is simultaneously thinking about grip, set-up, ball placement, takeaway, shoulder turn, knees, hips, watching the ball, and more. By the time his club actually connects with the ball, he's already exhausted. In contrast, a professional's swing is second nature, powered by the unconscious mind. Both demonstrate competence, but the professional's results are markedly superior.

I Think, Therefore I Think

Please take a few minutes to identify three skills you'd like to elevate from your current state of Conscious Competence to that of Unconscious Competence.

Your skills might include playing a musical instrument beautifully, conducting business, playing a sport, or even being an attentive spouse. When you've identified the skills, write them below:

1. _____

2. _____

3. _____

Look at your list and consider what it would mean to achieve true mastery of these skills. For example, think about what's involved in reading this page. Your eyes go over each word, your brain processes what the word means, and you instantly go on to the next word. It happens seamlessly, without conscious effort.

Your eyes know what to do, your brain knows what to do, and letters are immediately transformed into thoughts in your mind. This is the magic of achieving the state of Unconscious Competence.

In contrast, if you're learning a new language, every step of your reading requires conscious thought. First you read the word; then you consider whether you know what it means; then, if you do, you tell your brain to grab the translation for you; and finally you move on to the next word. When you reach the end of the sentence, you may need to go back and reconstruct what it means overall. You're able to read entire paragraphs this way, and even entire books; but the level of effort required is immense.

Another example comes from my own experience in martial arts. I'm a student of Brazilian Jiu-Jitsu. While I've trained extensively, I must continually use conscious thought to execute most of the moves. In contrast, my teacher, Carlson Gracie Jr., has attained the state of Unconscious Competence with his Jiu-Jitsu. He has what athletes call *muscle memory*. His skills are so ingrained that he vanquishes his opponents with seeming effortlessness and little conscious thought.

When I spar with him, I feel as if I'm trying to fight off an angry lion. I expend a tremendous amount of energy in our sessions. My breathing is heavy. I sweat. When the match is over, I'm ready for a nap. I feel like I've just been mauled. But Carlson is relaxed and unaffected. Without missing a beat, he proceeds to take on his next opponent.

This is your goal—master at least one area of your life so you're able to impose your will without effort and with full confidence in your abilities.

The single most effective way to move from Conscious Competence to Unconscious Competence is practice. So identify one skill that's most important to you, and then perform it again and again until it becomes a part of who you are.

Very few people achieve full mastery over any aspect of their lives beyond what their brains and bodies learned to do by the age of seven. Rise above the crowd. Become *automatic* in a meaningful way. You'll be amazed at the power and confidence that results.

Stage Four: Unconscious Competence

The final stage in the Four Stages of Learning is *Unconscious Competence*. It has the following characteristics:

- Over time, you've improved upon your strengths and abilities to handle challenges with such commitment and diligence that it enters the unconscious parts of your brain.
- Your strengths and problem-solving abilities have become second nature, enabling you to realize your desired results without conscious effort.
- You can demonstrate strengths and handle problems while engaged in other activities.
- You've mastered your strengths and problem-solving skills well enough to be able to teach them to others (unless, of course, teaching doesn't happen to be one of the strengths you possess).

When you're at the stage of Unconscious Competence, your strengths and problem-solving abilities have become an integral part of who you are. Those who master life at this level can appear magical to the rest of the world—because they make something look easy that almost everyone else finds very difficult to do.

I refer to this stage of learning as *the automation zone*. Engaging in your top skills or handling problems will be as second nature to you as breathing.

Life in *The Zone*

To understand what life in a state of Unconscious Competence looks like, consider the world's top athletes. If you're a Chicago Bulls fan, you may remember Michael Jordan in Game One of the NBA Finals against the Portland Trailblazers in 1992. Jordan lit up the Blazers for 35 points and made six three-pointers in the *first half* of the game.

One of the most unforgettable moments of that evening occurred after Jordan hit his sixth three-point shot. He simply shrugged his shoulders and raised his palms up by his sides as if to say "I can't explain it" as he back-trotted toward half-court. Playing the game that evening required almost no conscious thought for Jordan. He didn't expend any unnecessary energy contemplating what he would do when the ball came to him. The process was swift and efficient. He'd get the ball, place himself in position to take the shot, release the ball . . . and score. It was astoundingly simple.

After the game, Jordan was asked about his record-breaking evening. He referred to his performance as "being in the zone." It was, but that's really another way of saying he was operating from a state of Unconscious Competence.

We're drawn to those who demonstrate "zone-like" abilities. The world's best musicians pack concert halls. Authors who engage our imaginations sell hundreds of thousands of books. Top actors can earn millions for performing in a movie. The world values those who achieve a state of Unconscious Competence. If you follow this path, you may be able to powerfully affect an enormous number of people.

Living in a State of Unconscious Competence

Engaging in events and interactions while operating in a state of Unconscious Competence feels effortless and fulfilling. The periods of achieving this state tend to be rare, but you can increase their frequency by practicing your key skills. If you focus on achieving Unconscious Competence in even one area of your life, you'll begin the process of living in this magical state more often in other areas as well.

For example, consider the Dalai Lama. He communicates from a natural state of being, without pretense or overt effort. While he's conscious of his interactions with others, his words come straight from his heart. It's clear that he has eliminated those elements of his life that do not serve him well and achieved mastery over the ones that do.

The point isn't that you should become another Dalai Lama, but that you have the opportunity to redesign your life to meet whatever goals you set. It all begins with attaining the stage of Unconscious Competence in a single key skill. Once you do so, you'll have taken a critical step toward replicating the "automation zone" for an unlimited number of areas in your life. Plus you'll find yourself wanting to experience this way of being as often as possible.

The Four Stages of Learning: Summary

The Four Stages of Learning provides powerful tools for understanding and reinventing yourself. To truly own your life, you must be clear about who you are and why you do what you do.

Getting past Unconscious Incompetence means opening your eyes to forces from the past that drive you and recognizing strengths that propel you toward your destiny. By leveraging your natural Gifts and recognizing issues you've unknowingly battled day after day, you give yourself the ability to redefine your identity and behavior.

Conscious Incompetence and Conscious Competence are about choosing what to do with the qualities embedded deep within you that you're now consciously aware of. They give you the opportunity to hone in on innate talents and solve problems by perfecting pertinent skills.

Once you embark on this path, your goal is to reach the stage of Unconscious Competence. This will allow you to act effortlessly and effectively; and to be in touch with yourself and achieve peace and prosperity. Ultimately, you'll be able to do certain things so well that your abilities may appear to be magical.

The next step in your process of reinvention is to understand the importance that *The Pinnacle* plays in maximizing your ability to live life at the peak of your existence. Let's head to the summit.

The Next Stages of Learning—Takeaways

Conscious Incompetence

- You know your strengths but haven't yet fully leveraged them.
- You know your problems but haven't yet eliminated them.
- You must weigh the time and energy required to achieve competency in any given area against the benefits of doing so.
- Whatever choice you make, you're in a state of awareness . . . and in control of your life.

Conscious Competence

- You have the skills to effectively leverage your strengths and address your problems, but doing so still requires substantial conscious effort.
- To become "automatic" in exercising your skills, you must practice to reach Stage Four—Unconscious Competence.

Unconscious Competence

- Your strengths and problem-solving abilities have become second nature, enabling you to complete tasks without conscious effort.
- Becoming a master of even one area of your life is likely to result in great spiritual and psychological benefits.
- You're applauded and generously compensated when you become a master of your craft and inspire others.

WHAT IS YOUR *WHAT?*
Case Study #4: Robin Jay

Robin Jay is the writer, producer, and costar of the award-winning film, *The Keeper of the Keys*, as well as an author, and motivational speaker. Based in Las Vegas, she is also the founder of the Las Vegas Convention Speakers Bureau and a frequent media guest.

For the first 20 years of her career, Robin thrived in advertising sales. While the compensation was appealing, her body began to manifest health issues, a reflection of her unhappiness and lack of personal fulfillment. She knew she needed to make drastic changes and devised an exit strategy that included writing her first book, *The Art of the Business Lunch*.

Since 2005, she has released additional titles, published a bestselling anthology series, and in 2008, appeared in a lackluster personal development film. Seeking to elevate the genre as a whole, Robin began a three-year project to create an outstanding, funny personal development film. In 2011, *The Keeper of the Keys*, starring Jack Canfield, John Gray, and Marci Shimoff opened to a sold-out Las Vegas audience and has subsequently won the Las Vegas Film Festival award for Best Independent Film and the INDIE Fest award for Best Documentary, and is now in distribution. Robin is currently working on her next film, *The Secrets of the Keys*, which will star Brian Tracy, John Assaraf, and Mariel Hemingway.

Robin is a **Reinventor** and her *WHAT* is defined below. Visit TheKeyMovies.com for more information.

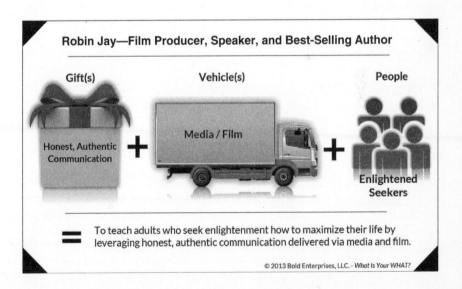

Robin Jay—Film Producer, Speaker, and Best-Selling Author

Gift(s)	Vehicle(s)	People
Honest, Authentic Communication	Media / Film	Enlightened Seekers

= To teach adults who seek enlightenment how to maximize their life by leveraging honest, authentic communication delivered via media and film.

© 2013 Bold Enterprises, LLC. - *What Is Your WHAT?*

The Pinnacle

Man is made or unmade by himself.
By the right choice, he ascends.
As a being of power, intelligence, and love,
and the lord of his own thoughts,
he holds the key to every situation.

—Sir James Allen

Design Your Ideal Life

When you're at your best, fully thriving, and living in a way that's consistent with who you were born to be, you've achieved what I call *The Pinnacle*.

The Pinnacle is living at the peak of your existence.

Imagine living without compromise. Imagine fulfilling your dreams and desires, surrounding yourself with people you love, and engaging in activities that bring you the most joy. What would you do each day if you could design your life in any way you choose?

Take a few moments to think about this. I want you to dream.

Now, dream big.

Now, dream even bigger.

Assume there are no barriers to what you want.

If your optimal life is touring the world, then picture yourself sailing on your 300-foot yacht. If it's playing golf every day, then envision yourself playing

18 holes in the morning and 18 in the afternoon. If it's being married to someone you deeply love, having two wonderful kids, and being the CEO of a well-respected company, then create that image in your mind.

Don't hold back. This is your ideal life. Design it however you like, without fear or limits. When you're ready to describe what your optimal life looks and feels like, please do so in the space that follows:

_____

_____

_____

_____

_____

_____

_____

_____

_____

_____

Designing your ideal life is a powerful exercise that enables your soul to soar without restrictions. You may find that once you begin the first sentence, your hand can't write fast enough as your subconscious kicks in and demands you recognize what's most important. This happens because you seldom give yourself the Gift of identifying what would bring you meaningful pleasure and happiness.

It's not your fault. The education you received at school hasn't prepared you adequately for living an outstanding life. While you can read, write, and solve mathematical equations, you were never taught to strive for, and thrive at, the peak of your existence.

But that's okay . . . because you'll learn to do so now.

If you were honest, what you've just written reflects your deepest needs—so heed it. You have the ability to create the life you want and live at The Pinnacle.

Before you can begin the process of reclaiming your summit, however, it's important to understand how you were knocked down from your perch.

The Downward Slide

You were born with extraordinary Gifts uniquely yours to harness, cultivate, and share with the world. As a baby and toddler, and even into adolescence, these talents were displayed raw and unrefined.

As you grew older, though, you likely encountered events that caused you to lose sight of some, or even all, of your natural capabilities. These events led you to adjust your identity, moving you away from who you truly are.

Examples of such personality-altering events include:

- Being chastised for acting "inappropriately"
- Being physically punished for displaying aspects of yourself that ran counter to someone else's beliefs or tastes
- Trying out for something (the football team, the high school play) and getting rejected
- Asking someone out on a date and being told no
- Having a room full of students cruelly laugh at you for something you did
- Being discouraged by friends or family from pursuing your dreams
- Enduring emotional or physical abuse

No matter what age you were when the events that affected you happened, you were quick to recognize that behavior X resulted in pain Y. This was all it took for you to bury that particular way of being under piles of emotional baggage.

Physical and emotional anguish subsides over time. The real tragedy is when you never fully reclaim the part of your personality lost during such incidents. An integral part of who you are is banished to the nether regions, never to be seen or heard from again by anyone . . . including you.

That may sound dramatic, but it's one of the realities of life. You do something that's naturally part of who you are, and if you're slapped down for it, you react. Too often, what gives way is your willingness to expose yourself again to the emotional or physical discomfort you experienced.

> *Each time you relinquish a piece of your core identity,*
> *you move further away from The Pinnacle.*

I call this process of descent *The Downward Slide*.

Traumatic events aren't the only factor. Another contributor is performing what you perceive as your duty. Whether you had a paper route, shoveled snow, or worked for your family's business, you did what you believed was required of you. It may be that what began as a way to bring in some extra cash became a straight line to a career path—even if it was work in which you had no genuine interest.

Or it could be that you accumulated so much debt from your schooling that you took whatever job you could find after graduation. It could also be that you turned your life upside down to accommodate your boyfriend, girlfriend, or spouse. Your good intentions for doing what was right, necessary, or expected of you became the grease on which you began your slide away from pursuing your true talents and passions—and away from The Pinnacle.

Once you begin the freefall, it's very difficult to reestablish your footing. Here's a typical scenario:

1. You go away to attend college.

2. Upon your return, you want to have your own place because that's what college grads do.

3. You take on a job, *any* job, so that you can afford your own place.

4. Bills start to pile up—school loans, utilities, cars, insurance, rent, furniture—not to mention the expenses of actually living life, such as food, hobbies, and dating.

5. You finally make a bit of money and you're feeling pretty good, so you buy a nicer car, move to a nicer place, wear better clothes, date higher-maintenance people.

6. Now that you have these nicer things, you must continue to work *hard* to pay for all of them.

7. You get married. You have kids.

8. You now have more mouths to feed and more responsibility on your shoulders.

9. You now have to work harder than ever just to cover your expenses. This might mean working overtime or taking on a second job.

10. The more you look at yourself in the mirror, the less you recognize who you are.

Chances are the job you started in Step 3 had nothing to do with fulfilling your deepest desires or pursuing happiness. It was simply the most convenient route at the time for making money, with the goal of eventually becoming self-supporting and putting yourself in a position to pursue your dreams.

This self-created fantasy is wonderful, but the reality is often more of a nightmare. After submitting to that first soul-deadening job, the downward slide away from The Pinnacle increasingly picks up momentum.

> *While everyone has to pay the bills, too few of us end up in professions even remotely resembling our dream jobs.*

Family and monetary obligations can run deep, and it's certainly possible to feel you had no choice but to do what was required of you or to maintain the lifestyle you created. That said, you must own the fact that from this point forward, you are making a conscious choice to continue living this way. You can't blame others for the life you've picked. If you're working in a dead-end job, it's because you choose to be there. If you're with someone you know is wrong for you, you're not making the effort to leave and find someone who's right. If you wake up miserable every day because of an event that occurred 30 years ago, you're making a decision to allow what happened in the past to control the quality of your life today.

You must begin to fight tooth and nail to reclaim your life and pursue what's most important to you.

The first step may be as simple as giving yourself the time and permission to sit in a quiet place and start trying to identify your Pinnacle. Some people need to hit rock bottom before realizing they've been on a continuous downward slide. Don't let that happen to you. Stop your descent right now. You have the power to ascend towards and reclaim The Pinnacle. The rest of this chapter will show you how.

Maslow Meets The Pinnacle

In 1943, psychologist Abraham Maslow famously hypothesized a *Hierarchy of Needs* that must be met before your ultimate state of existence—which he called *self-actualization*—can be reached. Maslow visualized the hierarchy as a pyramid (see Figure 5.1).

Maslow's Hierarchy of Needs has five distinct levels: physiological, safety, love/belonging, esteem, and self-actualization. These are genuinely powerful aids for understanding human behavior. However, Maslow believed that your physiological needs must be satisfied before you can move on to address safety

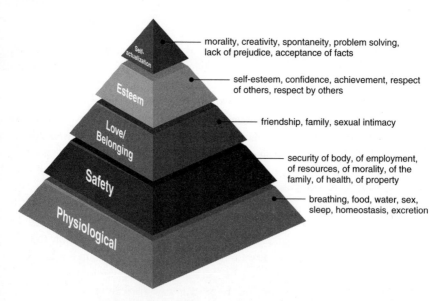

Figure 5.1   Maslow's Hierarchy of Needs

needs; your safety needs must be secured before you pursue love/belonging needs; and so on. He claimed that it's only when you fulfill the first four levels of needs that you can pursue self-actualization.

I disagree.

From Nelson Mandela to Che Guevara, there are numerous examples of self-actualized people who meaningfully affected the world and lived their life at The Pinnacle without having met all five levels of needs defined by Maslow. I'm therefore suggesting a different way of visualizing human needs, illustrated by the *Pinnacle Pyramid* shown in Figure 5.2.

The major difference between Maslow's Theory and mine is I contend the quality of your life is equally affected by each of the five levels. The Pinnacle serves as the stabilizing element for your life as a whole and enables you to thrive atop the delicate apex upon which your life balances. To live your life in this optimal state of being, you must become highly focused on the choices you make. Decisions that are incongruent with who you really are can easily send you flying off the summit—and send your Pyramid toppling to the ground.

The key to effective living is to first identify what most directly reflects The Pinnacle for you at each of the five levels of needs, and then apply The Pinnacle to your pursuit of those needs.

The following exercise will enable you to construct your own Pinnacle Pyramid. Doing so will help you understand what's most important to you, compare and contrast your current behavior with your answers, and provide a guideline for living that you can refer to and follow.

Let's begin.

Level One

Your physiological needs consist of breathing, food, water, sex, sleep, homeostasis, and excretion.

This may seem simple enough. But the choices you make in satisfying these needs spell the difference between living an ordinary life and living at The Pinnacle. To begin to understand this difference, please think about the following questions, and compare your answers with your behavior:

- What types of food are you most comfortable eating?
- What liquids do you most like to drink?
- What kinds of exercise do you enjoy?
- Does yoga or other breathing-related exercise fulfill you?
- How many hours of sleep are ideal for you?

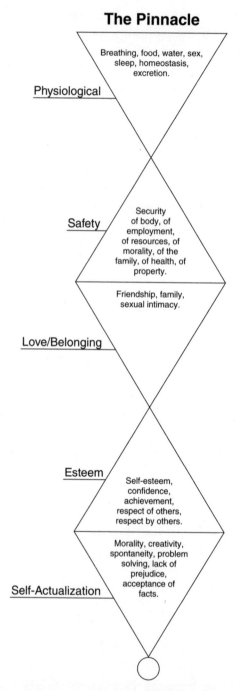

Figure 5.2   The Pinnacle Pyramid

Level Two

Your safety needs involve security of body, employment, resources, morality, the family, health, and property.

Being clear on the impact these needs have on you will help you maintain balance. Please consider how your responses to the following questions compare with your behavior:

- Do you feel the need for physical self-confidence? If so, do you practice martial arts or other physical activities that inspire a sense of safety in the event of an emergency? If not, do you instead practice sharpening your mental ability to get you out of dangerous situations?

- Does your job reflect your identity and passions? (There will be more about this in Part III, "Become Who You Were Born to Be.")

- Do your actions reflect your morality? For example, if you consider yourself religious, does your business and social behavior reflect your beliefs? Do you regularly attend a place of worship? If you aren't religious, do you consistently follow your own moral code?

- If your family is of the utmost importance to you, do you demonstrate this by the way you treat your loved ones?

- What do you do to ensure your physical well being? For example, do you exercise, and avoid smoking and stress?

- Do you maintain your home well? Do you beautify it? Do you pay your mortgage or rent on time?

Level Three

Your need for love and belonging consists of friendship, family, and sexual intimacy. Your needs on this level may have been damaged by your past, but Chapter 2's "The Vortex of Vulnerability" should have helped you become aware of these issues and begin the process of getting past them.

With that in mind, please think about the following questions, and compare your answers with your behavior:

- What's most important to you in a friendship? Do you need a large circle of friends, or do you prefer one or two very close friends? How often do you like to see your friends? How often do you like to talk to them?

- Is your family an integral part of your life? Is your immediate family of overriding importance to you, or is maintaining close relationships with your extended family also important? Do you see your family as often as possible, or do you create space to spend time apart?

- Do you prefer to have intimate sex or casual sex? Do you seek monogamy or prefer having multiple partners? Are you clear on your sexual needs and desires?

Level Four

Your need for esteem consists of self-esteem, confidence, achievement, respect of others, and respect by others.

Please consider the following questions and compare your behavior with your answers:

- From where do you derive your self-esteem? What do you need in order to feel good about yourself?

- How do you maintain a strong degree of confidence? Do you require continuous validation from others, or are you able to establish self-confidence without looking outside of yourself?

- How do you judge your achievements? On how much money you make? On the number of close, loving relationships you have? On helping those in need?

- Are you intimidated by or envious of the success of others? Does working with successful people make you think about all that's wrong with your world? Or does being around those who excel inspire you to achieve greatness?

- Do you yearn for the respect of everyone, for the respect of a select few, or just for your own self-respect? Do you judge people by how high they jump when you tell them to? Do you feel less worthy if people don't compliment you on your accomplishments?

Level Five

Your need for self-actualization involves morality, creativity, spontaneity, problem solving, lack of prejudice, and acceptance of facts.

Maslow defined self-actualization as "the full realization of one's potential; the desire for self-fulfillment, namely the tendency for the individual to become actualized in what he is potentially." It's at this level, according to Maslow, where you have complete freedom to soar.

Keeping this in mind, please think about the following questions, and compare your answers to your behavior:

- What are your guiding principles? Why do you believe you're here?
- How are you most creative? Do you like working with your hands? Do you love music? Does solving complex mathematical equations inspire you? Does coming up with new games to play with your kids make you happy?
- Are you spontaneous? Do you like to try new things? Can you adapt to changing circumstances? Or do you thrive on planning?
- Do you enjoy helping others with their problems? Do you achieve a state of fulfillment from finding a solution to something others could not figure out?
- Do you enjoy taking on all that comes your way without preconceived notions or fear driving your choices? Do you thrive on each of us being unique? At the same time, do you see past differences to a common humanity?
- Are you most at peace when life just *is*? Do you question everything that crosses your path, or do you take pride in the fact that it has chosen to share its existence with you in that moment? Do you consistently want to persuade others to see your point of view?

By examining the five levels of needs within the context of The Pinnacle, you can gain valuable insights into what matters most to you. You can then construct a personalized outline for living focusing on those areas.

My completed Pinnacle Pyramid is shown in Figure 5.3.

Think about your answers to the preceding questions, and use them to construct your own Pinnacle Pyramid. Keep your statements as concise as possible, yet detailed enough to represent your deepest needs and desires.

Use the blank template that follows to complete your personal Pinnacle Pyramid.

Alternatively, visit www.WhatIsYourWhat.com/resources to download the Pinnacle Pyramid template (see Figure 5.4), which will allow you to print out as many copies as you require.

Use your Pinnacle Pyramid as a convenient reference tool to help you achieve and maintain a solid foundation whenever the winds of change threaten to move you off your path.

Attaining The Pinnacle is incredibly challenging. The climb up the mountain is steep, and the terrain is far from smooth.

Achieving The Pinnacle is absolutely possible, though. In fact, at some point in your life, you were already there.

Now that you're aware of how you were knocked down from your peak and understand how to reclaim the summit, nothing should prevent you from taking flight and ascending to your most natural state of being.

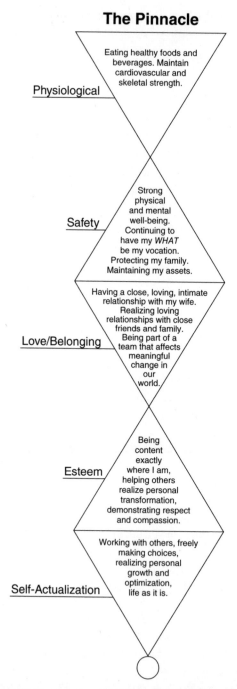

Figure 5.3   Steve's Completed Pinnacle Pyramid

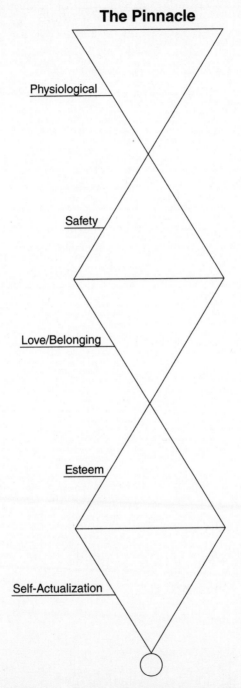

Figure 5.4   The Pinnacle Pyramid Template

The Pinnacle—Takeaways

- The Pinnacle is living at the peak of your existence.
- Each time you relinquish a piece of your core identity, you move further away from The Pinnacle.
- Reaching The Pinnacle is attainable. In fact, at some point in your life, you were already there.
- Being aware of how you were knocked down from your peak is the first step in ascending toward your most natural state of being.
- Stop the downward slide.
- The Pinnacle Pyramid can serve as a reference tool to help you maintain a solid foundation when the winds of change threaten to move you off your path.

Word Is Bond

Completing the process of establishing your foundation isn't possible until you gain a solid understanding of how your word affects who you are. To move your life forward, you must fulfill your commitments. Otherwise, nothing you build upon your new foundation will hold firm.

In 1990, rap star LL Cool J introduced the mainstream world to the term *word is bond* in his song "The Boomin' System" ("cause I'm frontin' in my ride and my word is bond"). The term stems from financial stock and bond markets in which transactions happened so quickly that traders had to work from verbal commitments. It was understood that at the end of the trading day they'd stand 100 percent by their deals, always upholding their word.

You must conduct yourself the same way—and in *all* areas of your life. If you promise to be a kind, compassionate, and loving father, always behave that way. If you promise to get X done by Y time, get it done. If you make a mistake, own up to it, and do whatever it takes to fix it.

Your word is who you are. Make your word your bond.

Establish the Foundation—In Closing

Congratulations on completing Part I of *What Is Your WHAT?*

Mastering The Four Stages of Learning, entering The Vortex of Vulnerability, taking on The Vortex of Invincibility, and ascending to The Pinnacle are not easy tasks. I commend you for your commitment to completing the most difficult section of this book.

You should now have a substantially better understanding of who you are and why you do what you do. I hope it's clear that the positive choices you make directly support your desired way of being . . . and vice versa.

You hold the power to choose what to do in every moment and, as you now know, there are only two choices:

1. Continue the descent, or

2. Stop the slide and ascend to the summit.

In which direction will you go?

Before moving on to Part II, where you'll be introduced to *The Seven Life-Altering Principles*, please take a few minutes to review the exercises, your answers, and any material you didn't fully absorb.

If any aspects of Part I were unclear, please take the time to reread those sections. Achieving thoughtful, rich understanding and leaving nothing to assumptions is a fundamental part of your reinvention process.

After you review the Takeaways for Establish the Foundation and are ready, proceed to Part II.

Establish the Foundation—Takeaways

- To live the life you deserve and desire, first Establish the Foundation.
- The Four Stages of Learning are powerful tools you can leverage to aid your understanding of who you are and why you do what you do.
- Set anchors deep into your soul. Be clear about what your path is and don't allow yourself to be blown off course by the whims of others.
- Don't let the "old you" come back and overthrow everything you've learned.
- Though you can learn from the past, it's largely irrelevant. In every current moment, you hold the power to choose what to do.
- You can design, create, and manifest your ideal life. Master your life instead of letting life master you.
- Achieving The Pinnacle is absolutely possible. In fact, at some point in your life, you were already there.
- Make the conscious choice to continue your descent or stop the slide and ascend to the summit.
- Your word is your bond. Say it, write it, do it, live it.

WHAT IS YOUR *WHAT?*
Case Study #5: Jenn Lim

Jenn Lim is the CEO and Chief Happiness Officer of Delivering Happiness, a company she and Tony Hsieh (CEO of Zappos) cocreated in 2010 to inspire happiness in work, community, and everyday life. She began her career as an Internet Strategist for KPMG, one of the world's largest consulting companies. After being laid off when the tech sector imploded and then losing her father to colon cancer, she contemplated what she desired to accomplish without the fear of failure or money driving her choices.

Her journey led her toward graphic design, writing, film, and . . . attempting to ascend Mt. Kilimanjaro. During her climb, she became clear that her interests lie in decoding the mysteries that shroud both corporate and personal potential for attaining one's higher purpose while sustaining happiness. In 2005, she created the first Culture Book for Zappos as a reflection of her findings and has produced them ever since. The Culture Book has become a global symbol for successfully creating an enjoyable, yet highly profitable, company.

In 2010, Jenn led the launch and management of Tony's best-selling book, *Delivering Happiness*. Building from the success of *The Culture Book* and *Delivering Happiness*, Jenn speaks and consults extensively on the subjects of Inspiration, Culture Change, and Happiness.

Jenn is a **Reinventor** and her *WHAT* is defined below. Visit DeliveringHappiness.com for more information.

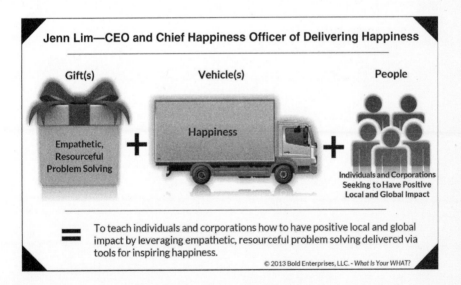

Jenn Lim—CEO and Chief Happiness Officer of Delivering Happiness

Gift(s)	Vehicle(s)	People

Empathetic, Resourceful Problem Solving

Happiness

Individuals and Corporations Seeking to Have Positive Local and Global Impact

= To teach individuals and corporations how to have positive local and global impact by leveraging empathetic, resourceful problem solving delivered via tools for inspiring happiness.

© 2013 Bold Enterprises, LLC. - *What Is Your WHAT?*

Realize Permanent, Positive Change

The Seven Life-Altering Principles (The S.L.A.P.)

The past is gone, the future yet unborn.
But right here and now is where it all goes on.

—Beastie Boys

Your power to influence yourself will always be enormously greater than your power to influence others. Even though it may seem like it at times, the world is not out to get you . . . nor does it revolve around you. However, if you allow yourself to become complacent, you'll end up somewhere you didn't intend to go.

Spending time complaining while you behave in ways that don't serve you well is self-destructive. Creating positive change in your life starts with making thoughtful decisions about your actions.

How different would your life be if you established guidelines for your actions that reflected your true nature? How powerful would you feel knowing you're focused on living your optimal life?

Can you picture yourself with this type of power and confidence? Can you imagine pursuing your life's objectives without fear of self-sabotage?

You can do all this, and more, by learning *The Seven Life-Altering Principles* and making them a part of who you are.

Realize Permanent, Positive Change

It's a scientific fact that we can undergo harmful genetic transformations—for example, debilitating mutation caused by exposure to toxic substances. But positive, permanent change is also possible. By harnessing the strength of your mind, you can overpower the genetic limitations of your physical body, and the damage caused by emotional and physical trauma.

A 2009 study at McGill University found that methylation—that is, genetic mutation brought on by negative stressors such as neglect or abuse—can be reversed by proactive measures, such as a positive environment coupled with psychotherapy. The latter combination has been shown to produce positive chemical changes in the brain.

The Seven Life-Altering Principles are designed to create a similar effect. By embracing them, you can reclaim the person you were born to be.

Entering Uncharted Territory

Reading *What Is Your WHAT?* from cover to cover in an uninterrupted fashion should never be your goal. It's not unusual for someone to spend a few days exploring a single principle. Many of the principles may lead you into unfamiliar, emotionally difficult territory. If this happens, don't be afraid.

Taking on new emotions, interactions, and activities that lead you into an uncomfortable state of being should be received with an open heart. Entering what you may perceive to be dangerous territory is really your mind and emotions expanding into unexplored lands. When you feel discomfort, acknowledge it, say "thank you," and proceed on your journey. Remain committed to evicting the limiting boundaries you've unconsciously put into place and move proactively towards becoming a new you.

Are you familiar with the saying "Wherever you go, there you are?" While it has been quoted by many, it actually dates back to the year 1441, when Thomas à Kempis wrote, "Wherever you go, you are burdened with yourself. Wherever you go, there you are."

To live the extraordinary life you deserve, you must commit to realizing positive, permanent change. You simply cannot run from who you are.

You can, however, become exactly who you want to be. The choice is yours . . . and the world awaits.

The Seven Life-Altering Principles — Takeaways

- Your power to influence yourself will always be enormously greater than your power to influence others.
- You can heal emotional and physical trauma.
- Be willing to put yourself in a state of emotional discomfort to move beyond your perceived limitations.
- Wherever you go, there you are.

WHAT IS YOUR *WHAT*?
Case Study #6: Guy Kawasaki

Guy Kawasaki is the cofounder of Alltop.com, founding partner at seed and early-stage venture capital firm Garage Technology Ventures, special advisor to the Motorola unit at Google, and previously, Chief Evangelist at Apple. A popular speaker and author of numerous books including *Enchantment*, *What the Plus!* and *APE: How to Publish a Book*, Guy is one of the Internet's most recognized and influential icons with ~4,000,000 Google+ followers, 1,300,000 Twitter followers, and ~300k Facebook fans.

After graduating from Stanford and receiving his MBA from UCLA, Guy began his career in jewelry marketing. There, he learned how to sell—a skill he credits with being a vital component of his future business success. Several years later, he was introduced to the Apple computer and technology immediately became a permanent fixture in his life.

He eventually landed a job with Apple and began evangelizing Macintosh to software and hardware developers. Over the subsequent years, Guy received an honorary doctorate from Babson College, created and sold multiple software companies and, later, returned to Apple as an Apple fellow. Along each step of his path, Guy has honored his ability to persevere and empower people in need of clarity and direction to attain their desired objectives.

Guy is a **Reinventor** and his *WHAT* is defined below. Visit GuyKawasaki.com for more information.

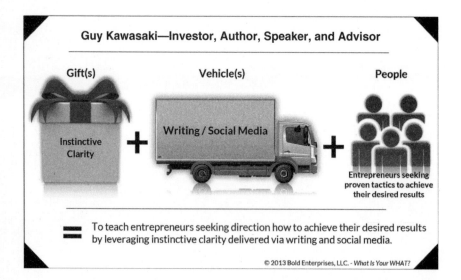

Guy Kawasaki—Investor, Author, Speaker, and Advisor

Gift(s)	Vehicle(s)	People
Instinctive Clarity	Writing / Social Media	Entrepreneurs seeking proven tactics to achieve their desired results

To teach entrepreneurs seeking direction how to achieve their desired results by leveraging instinctive clarity delivered via writing and social media.

© 2013 Bold Enterprises, LLC. - *What Is Your WHAT?*

Life-Altering Principle #1

YāNo

Your life is the sum result of all the choices you make, both consciously and unconsciously. If you can control the process of choosing, you can take control of all aspects of your life. You can find the freedom that comes from being in charge of yourself.

—Robert F. Bennett

Throughout your life, you've experienced thousands of life-altering events that were completely within your control. They all reflect choices you made—consciously or unconsciously. The resulting impact on your life is the foundation upon which the concept of *YāNo* (pronounced Yay-No) is built.

There are precise moments, which I refer to as *YāNo moments*, in which you either move toward growing and thriving, or digress in a direction that's inconsistent with your true self. A key to living a fulfilling and genuine life is taking control of these life-altering moments and choosing the paths that are beneficial for you.

YāNo is the principle of recognizing when you're faced with a "moment of truth" that will have meaningful impact on your life and making the choice that's the most appropriate and nourishing for you.

Please take a few minutes to reflect on your life and identify as many life-altering events as you can. These may include

- Graduating from college
- Getting married
- Breaking a limb
- The birth of your child
- Starting a new job
- Getting in a fistfight
- Crashing your car
- Making a game-winning shot

Many YāNo moments will be obvious, such as a marriage proposal. Others may seem insignificant if you aren't paying close attention. For example, you might agree to meet a friend for drinks even though you don't enjoy drinking. Or you might donate money to a politician who your boss supports but you secretly despise.

The more you agree to participate in activities that don't feel right, the more likely you are to feel your life is out of control. To avoid this, you must address each YāNo moment with equal seriousness.

This may be a hard concept to swallow. How can a bar invitation demand as much attention from you as a marriage proposal?

The answer is this: Any time you undertake an activity without evaluating the impact your choice will have on your life, you run the risk of compromising your state of mind.

Don't get me wrong. I'm not suggesting that you rigidly refuse any action about which you're not 100 percent gung-ho. But I want you to recognize that it's a YāNo moment.

The key to regaining control of your life is to make deliberate choices with an understanding of the consequences. Once you do, you'll stop childishly blaming others for your actions. If you choose to undertake an activity that makes you uncomfortable, at least you'll have consciously made the choice based upon review of your options. Being resentful of the person who asked you to perform the activity is misguided.

As you practice YāNo, you'll shift to focusing on the potential result of a decision (e.g., facing 60 payments at $500/month) whenever you're faced with a YāNo moment (e.g., buying a car you can't afford). As a result, you'll have a greater opportunity to base your actions on what is most true to who you inherently are.

Living with YāNo

Living the principle of YāNo is hard work because it requires you to be fully aware of the choices you make. But the more you learn to recognize YāNo moments, the easier it will become. To most effectively implement the principle of YāNo in your normal routine, do the following:

- Look for YāNo moments throughout your day. This tends to be the hardest part because you're probably in the habit of blowing past YāNo moments without thinking about them. However, learning to recognize these moments will have a profoundly positive impact on your life. To reinforce this learning, take a few minutes before you go to bed each night to note the most important YāNo moments you faced during that day.
- When confronted with a YāNo moment, slow down. Take the time to obtain a clear understanding of the situation—including what's expected of you and what's truly right for you.
- Identify each of your options. Recognize that there are often choices beyond *yes* or *no*, and consider alternatives to the obvious.
- Evaluate the consequences of each possible path. Try to envision the effect of your decision an hour from now, a month from now, and a year from now.
- Make a choice and then commit to it. After you've put the work into recognizing and evaluating the YāNo moment, step up and own your decision.
- Act on your choice with the strength of conviction. If you need to explain yourself, do so with empathy, but also firmness.

At first this process may be alarmingly uncomfortable; but that's true of almost any journey worth taking.

This may also require you to devote an extraordinary amount of time and energy when you start out. However, most people get the hang of it within just a couple of days. After that, your main challenge will be to reduce the amount of time required for you to work through the process.

Stick with it. As you incorporate the principle of YāNo into your everyday life, it will become increasingly easier; eventually it will become almost effortless.

An Example of a YāNo Moment

Not long ago, I faced a YāNo moment that could have had a significant negative impact on me if I hadn't clearly evaluated the situation and potential consequences. One path would have provided meaningful benefit to a friend and the accomplishment of his objectives, but would have led me down an uncomfortable road. Another path represented an opportunity to participate in my friend's wonderful cause while still being true to myself.

What led to the moment was a discussion regarding The Prosperity Project, a one-day seminar for high-school and college-age students designed to teach both financial literacy and the identification of a vocation one can pursue with zeal. I'm proud to be associated with this project, and I'm even more proud of my friend for creating it.

When he asked me to be a presenter, I instantly recognized it was a YāNo moment. I quickly weighed my options, decided that participating was in line with my nature and personal objectives, and told him I'd be glad to take part. My friend is very knowledgeable about economics and finance, and I'm an expert at helping people identify their *WHAT*, so I assumed he would handle the financial literacy aspect of the curriculum and I'd tackle the vocational component.

When we next got together, however, I realized that he'd interpreted our conversation to mean I was accepting responsibility for the *entire* presentation, both financial and vocational. I'd neglected to base my YāNo decision on a clear understanding of the other person's expectations. This misunderstanding created a second YāNo moment. To address it, I used the following process:

1. To avoid another misunderstanding, I asked my friend to articulate his expectations.

2. Based on a clear understanding of the situation, I formulated options. I came up with three:

   a. Tell him "thanks, but no thanks," and bail on the project.

   b. Agree to present the entire curriculum.

   c. Explain I was uncomfortable presenting the financial material, but would be happy to present the vocational component.

3. I evaluated these options, considering which one most closely aligned with my true nature and was most likely to produce positive results.

4. I chose option *c*.

5. I acted on my decision by informing my friend of my feelings and preferences.

After a few minutes of discussion, we agreed that he would handle the financial literacy presentation. This process took little effort. And because I was clear in communicating my decision and the reasons behind it, my friend felt no animosity and we proceeded to jointly create a terrific presentation.

However, had I not recognized the YāNo moment and just gone along with my friend's plans, it would have caused damage. First, the presentation wouldn't have been nearly as effective because I'm not an expert on finance. And second, I would have resented my friend for putting me in the uncomfortable position of doing his job for him and failing at it to boot. Both the students and our friendship inevitably would have suffered.

The You of Today Affects the You of Tomorrow

One of the most significant aspects of effectively managing your YāNo moments is making choices today that will have a positive impact on your future self, the *you of tomorrow*. When you think this way, you're less likely to apply for a job you know would be a terrible fit; eat greasy foods that make you feel awful afterward; say something in anger to a loved one that might permanently change the relationship; or drive when drunk, which risks completely ruining your future.

When faced with a YāNo moment, choose whatever option provides the most rewarding long-term benefits, allowing the you of tomorrow to look back and give thanks to the you of today.

Life-Altering Principle #1: YāNo—Takeaways

- Begin to recognize YāNo moments.

- Favor choosing the option that provides the most rewarding long-term benefits.

- YāNo makes difficult decisions easier as you move from being overly concerned with how you affect others to making choices that are most congruent with your soul.

- The key to regaining control of your life is to make deliberate choices with an understanding of the consequences.

- Shift to focusing on the potential result of a decision whenever you're faced with a YāNo moment.

- Allow the you of tomorrow to look back and give thanks to the you of today.

WHAT IS YOUR *WHAT*?
Case Study #7: Bill Renkosik

Bill Renkosik, aka Bad Boy Bill, is an international DJ and music producer who has been a mainstay on the electronic dance scene for almost 30 years. Consistently ranked among the elite of all global DJs, he has shared the stage with the world's most popular entertainers including Calvin Harris, David Guetta, Afrojack, Fat Boy Slim, Tiesto, and Paul Oakenfold.

Growing up in Chicago, Bill was first drawn to the allure of being a DJ after hearing The Hot Mix 5 blend House music records together on WBMX-FM. After viewing the pop-culture classic films *Breakin'* and *Beat Street*, he was officially hooked and convinced a friend to split the cost of two turntables, a mixer, and roughly a dozen records. Together, they practiced mixing and scratching day and night until Bill became good enough to land a position on Farley Jack Master Funk's radio show . . . at the age of 16.

Appearing on Chicago's most popular radio station helped Bill land hundreds of DJ gigs, which ultimately led to his creating and selling thousands of "mix tapes" out of the trunk of his car. Recognizing the opportunity to massively increase sales, Bill spearheaded an initiative to create his own record label, "legalize" the mix tape production process, and, eventually, secure distribution deals with leading retailers including Best Buy and Tower Records.

As the compilations hit the national scene, his popularity grew. This led to Bill receiving invitations to DJ at clubs all over the world and expanding his focus to include the production of original music. He remains an in-demand DJ, producer, and re-mixer to this day.

Bill is a **Birther** and his *WHAT* is defined below. Visit BadBoyBill.com for more information.

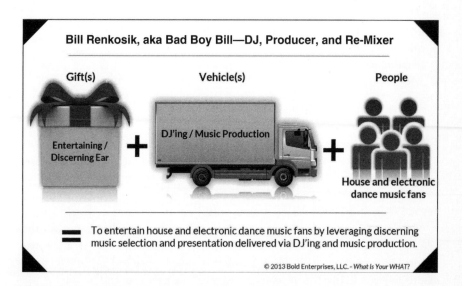

Bill Renkosik, aka Bad Boy Bill—DJ, Producer, and Re-Mixer

Gift(s)	Vehicle(s)	People
Entertaining / Discerning Ear	DJ'ing / Music Production	House and electronic dance music fans

= To entertain house and electronic dance music fans by leveraging discerning music selection and presentation delivered via DJ'ing and music production.

© 2013 Bold Enterprises, LLC. - *What Is Your WHAT?*

Life-Altering Principle #2

Reclaim the Canyon

Between stimulus and response, there is a space.
In that space is our power to choose our response.
In our response lies our growth and our freedom.

—Viktor E. Frankl

The interactions you face on a daily basis can often be trying. Some guy cuts you off in the middle of the highway. Your boss is on a rampage because the company just lost a big account, and your desk is located closest to his office. Your neighbor's dog ruined your prized rose bush. Many of these events are beyond your control, but what you *can* control is your response to them.

Most people focus on the times when things are being said or done, but the periods in between are just as critical. It's in these "areas of silence" that you can choose the best path for you. Leveraging this sacred space into a powerful asset will enable you to live the life you desire and *Reclaim the Canyon*.

Reclaim the Canyon is the principle of establishing space between life as it happens and your reaction to those events.

The Power of the Pause

When faced with adversity—such as missing a bus that makes you late for work or having a heated exchange with a friend—how do you normally react? Do you immediately let the incident take full control of your mind, body, and spirit? Is your day pretty much over from that point forward? Our reactions are often similar to how we step over a crack in the sidewalk. They happen swiftly, without thought, and with no regard for what we might be stepping into on the other side.

How different would your life be if your first response to an upsetting event was simply a pause—a long, thoughtful pause comparable in size to the Grand Canyon?

It's within this pause that you can quiet your emotions, gather your thoughts, and rationally consider the situation and the best way to respond to it.

Of course, a long pause is not always practical. There are times when an immediate response is vital, such as when a child is standing in the way of a speeding car. It's for these kinds of emergencies that we're wired to respond in a split second.

For most everyday situations, however, it's perfectly okay to meaningfully pause while you gather your thoughts. Many top communicators, such as President Barack Obama, are renowned for taking their time to consider internally many sides of an issue before articulating an opinion.

Knowing how long a pause to take and how to vary that pause appropriately depending on the complexity and scale of the issue involved, is a skill you'll develop over time. But the first and most important step is to change your reaction from instantaneous and thoughtless to becoming the result of meaningful consideration.

Communication as Manipulation

Avoid giving others the power to dictate the amount of time it takes you to respond. This is your sacred space. It's within this space that you have the power to maintain perspective. Without it, it's easy for others to manipulate you.

Both positive and negative communications are, at a basic level, efforts at manipulation. While this may sound cynical, the fact remains that you can't blindly accept anything at face value.

For example, when someone tells you "wow, you're cute," or "you're so smart," or "you did a really good job," the natural response is for every fiber in your being to light up. You instantly assume the person's intent is to make you feel good, and so you feel good about the communication.

However, other people sometimes have their own agenda when they issue a compliment. What if this person needs bus fare and he wants you to be in a positive mood before hitting you up for it? What if the person knows her current love interest is going to be walking by in a few minutes and she wants to engage you in conversation to make herself appear attractive? By not reacting instantly, you avoid allowing yourself to be controlled.

On the other hand, when someone tells you to "go to hell," your first instinct is to believe the person wants you to lose control and become angry, and, in most cases, you do. But what if this person had a really rough day and you just happened to be in the middle of her hailstorm? What if this person just lost his wallet and is in a state of panic? What if the person is mentally unstable? Maybe the appropriate response is to remain calm and not get involved in someone else's drama or possibly help the person regain a state of balance.

If you react instantly and obviously, you make it easy for others to manipulate you, and you shut out the possibility of a more nuanced and on-target response.

Of course, sometimes things are precisely as they appear. A friend might say something nice to you because she loves you. And a colleague might curse at you because he's truly upset.

Further, even if a communication is a blatant attempt at controlling your behavior, that doesn't mean you shouldn't go along with it. If the person is a friend or colleague, your interests will typically be aligned with what the person wants you to do.

The point is to be aware of what's happening and to make conscious choices. If you stop to consider before reacting to both positive and negative comments, you'll be in control of how the words of others make you feel about yourself.

Remember: pause first—speak second.

Take the Initiative

One of the key elements of successfully implementing the concept of Reclaim the Canyon is to take the initiative. Most people believe life simply happens and events are outside of their control. This is dangerously wrong. There are unquestionably times when random things happen, such as a hurricane or an act of terrorism. However, the majority of your experiences are within your control to guide and manage.

To effectively accomplish this objective, establish control of your experiences. This isn't as difficult as it may seem. For instance, assume you're driving your car to work. Seemingly out of nowhere, another driver crazily cuts in front of you and slams on the brakes. Your likely response is to become furious, start screaming obscenities, and let the incident ruin the rest of your day. You have totally responded to this experience.

Alternatively, you had the ability to take the initiative as you drove to work. You could've made the effort to be fully aware of your surroundings—checking your mirrors, taking careful notice of other drivers, and trying to anticipate what might intercept your path. In this scenario, you probably would've spotted the reckless driver sooner, and slowed down or switched lanes to avoid getting too close to the other car.

As another example, assume the company you own is on the verge of failing, but you have the opportunity to pitch a major client that could keep your firm in the black for the next two years. You can simply create the pitch based on your experience with previous clients, deliver it, and wait for the client to make his decision.

Alternatively, you can first talk with the client to make 100% sure that you understand his needs and desires. You can even make an initial presentation *before* the official pitch to receive feedback and ensure you're on track to seal the deal.

Granted, there may be times when you won't have access to key decision-makers. However, with enough creativity and determination, you can find ways to leave as little to chance as possible, stacking the odds in favor of your success.

> **Taking the initiative enables you to gain control of your life**
> **by reducing the effect of external forces.**

Leveraging the principle of Reclaim the Canyon will enable you to significantly reduce the apparent "randomness" in your world and empower you to embrace life with open eyes. By mitigating the effects of the actions of others, you'll avoid being at the mercy of their whims. And consciously maintaining awareness and control over interactions will help you prevent many negative events from ever happening.

Life-Altering Principle #2: Reclaim the Canyon—Takeaways

- Leverage the area of silence between what's being said and done to choose your best path.
- Change your reaction from being instantaneous and thoughtless to being the result of meaningful consideration.
- Avoid giving others the power to dictate the amount of time it takes you to respond.
- Pause first—speak second.
- Avoid being at the mercy of the whims of others by mitigating the effects of their actions.
- Take the initiative to prevent negative events from happening and increase the chance for realizing positive results.
- Side-step life's continuous drama barrage, and handle each moment in an appropriate manner.

WHAT IS YOUR *WHAT?*
Case Study #8: Barry Sorkin

Barry Sorkin is the co-owner of Smoque BBQ, one of Chicago's most popular BBQ restaurants. Since opening its doors in late 2006, Smoque has garnered substantial press and rave reviews. A highlight includes a featured segment on Guy Fieri's *Diners, Drive-Ins & Dives* and high ratings from Zagat, DailyCandy, Urbanspoon, and Michelin.

Growing up skinny, white, Jewish, and without any family restaurant experience to lean on, Barry scarcely resembles the image conjured up by most when envisioning a typical BBQ purveyor. Coupled with his journalism degree and nearly a decade spent creating marketing materials for an IT consulting firm, nary an inkling of Barry's equation lends itself to predicting his future success as a restaurateur.

Yet, throughout his life, Barry's love for BBQ has remained front and center—an undeniable draw, and a hobby he contemplated forging a business around. Researching the subject extensively, he enrolled others in his vision and traveled to Memphis, Kansas City, North Carolina, and Austin to learn from many of the best BBQ chefs in the country. Recognizing his strengths and limitations, he secured four key partners with whom he could bring his idea to fruition.

Today, Smoque has a loyal following, its own BBQ sauce, and a systematic, controlled approach to growth. While myriad opportunities to expand are proposed daily, for now, the partners remain focused on serving up one extraordinary plate of BBQ at a time.

Barry is a *Reinventor* and his *WHAT* is defined below. Visit www.SmoqueBBQ.com for more information.

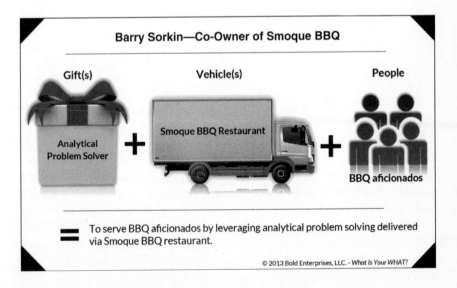

Barry Sorkin—Co-Owner of Smoque BBQ

Gift(s)	Vehicle(s)	People
Analytical Problem Solver	Smoque BBQ Restaurant	BBQ aficionados

= To serve BBQ aficionados by leveraging analytical problem solving delivered via Smoque BBQ restaurant.

Life-Altering Principle #3

The Sufficiency Theory

Do not spoil what you have by desiring what you have not.
Remember that what you now have was
once among the things you only hoped for.

—Epicurus

Many in the Western world are on a misguided mission of searching for the latest, greatest, shiniest, most desired pieces of crap that money can buy. Others won't rest until they have the biggest house, fanciest car, and largest bank account. Then the day comes when they attain what they've been pursuing. And what happens? Satisfaction and contentment kick in for a short while and then they begin the quest for the next item that is sure to provide fulfillment.

We've been programmed to believe that what we have is never good enough and we should constantly be striving for more. There's a destructive cultural correlation between the quality of our "things" and the quality of our lives. Yes, it's natural and healthy to want to better yourself. But our obsession with material possessions stems from Madison Avenue's advertising wizards, who adroitly lead us to define our sense of self by what we own.

That may be good for our economy. However, this mentality of dissatisfaction often carries over to our personal lives. Continually looking outside of yourself for your self-worth keeps you from getting in touch with your true needs and eliminates the possibility of generating happiness from within. Striving for external gratification prevents you from maintaining a feeling of contentment that stems from who you are and what you do.

The Sufficiency Theory exalts a way of life based on patience, perseverance, diligence, wisdom, moderation, and reasonableness. In other words, desire less and be less reliant on others. There's a direct relationship between self-reliance and achieving harmony and balance. By eliminating outside influences, you gain the power to leverage this powerful dynamic and reclaim your life.

The Sufficiency Theory is the principle of attaining satisfaction, peace, and contentment by minimizing material desires and the effect of outside influences.

The Utopian Myth

Many people operate on the belief that when they finally own X, make X amount of money, or have accomplished X as a career goal, they'll give themselves permission to take on certain activities that they expect will make them feel amazing. The result of this mind-set is they continually live for tomorrow without ever fully enjoying today.

Think back on your life. Have you ever drawn a line in the sand and said, "When I get to this point, everything I need will be perfectly in place and then I can really start living?" When you were 18, did you think to yourself, "If I can just get into the right college, my life will be perfect?" After you landed your first job, did you think to yourself, "I'll work really hard, and after I have X number of dollars in the bank I'll really be able to enjoy life?"

If so, when you finally reached that magical line, how often did you scratch it out and create another line further down the path? That's how most people in our Western world live. Our journey typically goes like this:

1. **We set our objectives:** We arbitrarily draw a line in the sand (e.g., buying a new house, earning X number of dollars per year), and from that point on we're controlled by our efforts to achieve those goals.

2. **We focus on meeting our objectives:** We put off things that we want (traveling, having a baby, contentment) until we meet our financial, career, or social goals.

3. **We believe achieving our objectives is the goal:** We expect the successful completion of the tasks we've set for ourselves will bring us unlimited satisfaction and launch us towards happiness.

4. **When we finally achieve our objectives, we set new ones:** We're happy for a short time. Then we draw a new line in the sand and return to being discontented and living for the future.

One of the key problems with this process is that we're always looking for external things—riches, fame, awards, validation—to provide internal satisfaction. Happiness is treated as some sort of destination that can be reached by attaining select milestones. And until that happens, we don't even try for pure, unabashed joy . . . or attempt to live out our heart's desire.

Beyond having enough to sustain your life, having X number of dollars or X possessions means very little. However, your internal dialogue associated with these things means a great deal. You can choose to give them power over your life, or you can own your happiness. You can choose to live within a state of satisfaction and contentment, or in a constant state of pause.

Here's the wake-up call: There's no magical place for you to reach at the end of your journey. Nothing incredible will happen when you achieve all of your objectives.

> *The utopia at the end of the rainbow—with flowing streams, beautiful people, a pot of gold, and eternal happiness—is a myth.*

To put this in perspective, imagine you want to get married. Each time you go on a date, you hide your true self because you don't want to expose the *real* you until you've been hitched. So on a date you're rude, say hurtful things, and are all-around bad company. When questioned about your conduct, you respond: "Don't worry, this isn't the real me. After we get married, I promise I'll be exactly the type of person you're hoping for." Needless to say, you have few second dates. No one wants to stick around to see who the *real* you actually is.

A second example comes from my presentations for job seekers. I speak extensively to people in transition, as my heart breaks for those who are finding it difficult to land on their feet. Part of my process includes asking attendees to provide adjectives that describe how they're feeling while out of work. Words such as *afraid, depressed, unworthy, embarrassed, ashamed, angry, disappointed,* and *disconnected* are commonly used. I then draw a line in the center of a whiteboard and place these words on the left-hand side:

Afraid	
Depressed	
Unworthy	
Embarrassed	
Ashamed	
Angry	
Disappointed	
Disconnected	

Next, I ask them to describe what happens to these emotions after they land a job. In other words, what does *afraid* become? What does *depressed* become? I then write their responses on the right side of the whiteboard:

Afraid	Unafraid
Depressed	Happy
Unworthy	Capable
Embarrassed	Proud
Ashamed	Confident
Angry	Content
Disappointed	Excited
Disconnected	Connected

I then ask how an interview might go if they enter the room carrying the burden of the emotions represented by the left side of the board. Most will say "not well," "there's no way you'd be hired," or something similar. I follow by asking how the interview might go if they enter the room with the lightness of the right side of the board lifting their spirit. Most respond "very well" and "odds are good of landing the job."

Pausing for a moment, I then ask what it costs to shift their state of mind to living the right column on a consistent basis. Someone always nails the answer—NOTHING. And what does it cost to remain in their current state of mind represented by the left side of the board? EVERYTHING.

*Shifting from the left side of the board to the right costs you absolutely
nothing, while not doing so costs you everything. This is an
investment worth making.*

This scenario is consistent with typical behavior. We deny ourselves the
benefit of the personality we believe we'd display until we reach the arbitrary
lines we've created.

If you live your life hoping that something miraculous will happen, what
is this process of postponement costing you? What are you not doing that you
otherwise would? Recognizing that the destination *is* the road and that the *journey*
is the destination spells the difference between living in a permanent state of
anticipation and living in a way that creates continuous satisfaction.

Being on the road is itself the victory. You've won. Don't pine for something in
the future. Relax and enjoy the ride. You are exactly where you're supposed to be.

The Sufficiency Paradigm Shift

In order to truly enjoy the journey, you must reverse the way people typically
pursue their objectives. I recommend the process described in the next three
sections.

Feel Content by Imagining You've Achieved Your Goals

The first step is to feel peace and contentment by imagining that you've already
achieved your objectives.

Whatever you've convinced yourself you'll feel once you accomplish certain
goals is the way you *must* start feeling from today on. This shift will powerfully
enable you to achieve your objectives from a foundation of happiness.

For example, if you believe X number of dollars in the bank will fulfill you,
I want you to imagine what having the money would feel like—and then
create that state of mind for yourself *right now*. (Those who practice the Law of
Attraction employ a similar approach.)

What would your posture be like? How often would you smile? How deeply
would you breathe? How would you treat others? What activities would you
pursue? Whatever your answers, adjust your current behavior to match them.

I want you to begin, this very moment, to live out the physiological results of
achieving your goals, and start to feel the emotions you've been putting off for
the future.

Obviously, you must deal with the constraints of reality. If traveling around
the world is one of your objectives and you have $25 to your name, that's not an

activity you can pursue right away. However, it costs you nothing to try to feel as if you've already traveled the world and to let that feeling of accomplishment be the foundation on which you operate.

Do Things Aligned with Who You Want to Become

The second step is to engage in activities that support the way you want to be.

Once you start operating with a positive attitude of accomplishment and a strong sense of self, amazing things happen. The choices you make and the activities you undertake will be markedly different from the way you used to live, and people will pick up on your aura of success, increasing your chances of achieving genuine success.

Further, you'll free yourself from the pressure of meeting certain objectives before you can feel and act in ways that are most natural for you. In other words, you're giving yourself permission to be who you really are.

Reach Your Goals

The third step is to achieve your objectives.

By feeling and acting like you've already succeeded, you inevitably *will* succeed . . . and sooner rather than later.

This three-step process is the polar opposite of the way we've been trained to achieve our objectives. However, it's much more effective.

In fact, many experts suggest you envision the end result you desire to help achieve it. Jim Carrey wrote himself a multimillion-dollar check for "Acting Services Rendered" and kept it in his wallet as a reminder of his goals long before he ever got his first big break. He envisioned what he wanted, and he knew that one day he'd be rewarded for his talents at his desired level of compensation.

The Sufficiency Theory is similar in approach. However, when you simply envision an outcome, you're putting off your feelings of fulfillment and contentment until the objective is met. The Sufficiency Theory doesn't stop at asking you to envision your goal; it asks you to live as if you've already achieved it . . . and to use that sense of being victorious as fuel for propelling you on your journey.

An Example of the Sufficiency Paradigm Shift

Putting The Sufficiency Theory into practice may be hard to imagine, so here's an example of the process in action.

***Desired objective and outcome: Have a baby and then we'll
be a happy family!***

For a family trained to think conventionally, the process might look something like this:

1. **We set our objectives:** We want to have a baby so that we can be a complete and happy family. To accomplish this, we need to have X number of dollars in the bank. Right now, things aren't where we want them to be. We know our life will be complete when we have our baby.

2. **We focus on meeting our objectives:** We work and work until we have X number of dollars in the bank. This might take one year, or it might take five. Until this objective is achieved, we live in a state of discontent because we don't have a baby and how can we be a happy family without a baby?

3. **We believe achieving our objectives is the goal:** Finally we have X number of dollars in the bank, and we start actively trying to have a baby. One year later, our baby is born. Having a baby turns out to be a lot of work and that little SASK (sleep and sex killer) sure is expensive to have around. The dollars in the bank start diminishing, and we feel tired all the time.

4. **Where is the utopia we imagined for ourselves?** The happiness we thought we'd have when the baby came is not magically appearing.

5. **We draw new lines in the sand:** We plan to replenish our funds so that we once again have X number of dollars in the bank. We also plan to return to sleeping through the night. Once these things happen, then we can really start being happy!

Is it clear how the typical process continually breeds discontent? When you're always looking outside of yourself for other people, places, or things to bring you joy, you'll never be happy for long. In order to live a life filled with sufficiency, you must begin to accept and love who you are and what you have.

Now let's look at how the same situation is handled under The Sufficiency Theory:

*Desired objective and outcome: Have a baby and then we'll
be a happy family!*

1. **Feel peace and contentment from imagining you've already achieved your objectives:** Life with my spouse is truly enjoyable. We talk, we share, we play, we love, we fight. Seeing my spouse brings me joy. Spending time with my spouse is one of my favorite things to do in the world. Our family is content. Our life together is meaningful as it is. We've chosen to have a baby and look forward to our new boy or girl being part of our family. Having a baby will only further enrich what is already a fulfilling life for us.

2. **Engage in activities that support the way you want to be:** We don't feel pressure to get pregnant. We don't need a baby in order to have peace and contentment. In this frame of mind, we perform the happy dance . . . often! One little swimmer hits the target, and we're on our way to having our baby. We also recognize that having a baby will increase our cost of living. One of us takes on a part-time job to help put additional money into our savings account.

3. **Achieve your objectives:** Nine months later, our baby is born. Since we don't rely on the baby to bring us peace and contentment, our experience in raising our child is markedly different from that of needing to have a child in order to be happy together. We benefit from this state of being. And our child benefits.

4. **Our family grows closer as time goes on:** We work together to take on the additional responsibilities of raising a child. It's trying and tiring at times, but our love and happiness help see us through.

Accepting the Sufficiency paradigm shift requires a substantial commitment because we're so used to expecting our peace and contentment to come from outside of ourselves.

I encourage you to start with your most important relationship—be it your spouse, your child, a parent, a sibling, or a best friend. Look at your relationship from a place of peace and contentment.

If you want to be happy with your spouse, as Dr. Laura Schlessinger says, "start now by becoming the kind of partner you'd want to come home to." Give the one you love a massage, cook dinner, encourage your spouse to take a long bubble bath, or pick up the dry cleaning. Whatever it is you know the love of your life wants, do it.

The idea is to shift your approach from waiting for certain things to happen, to feeling and acting in that manner *now* and enjoying this positive state of mind. You'll be amazed at how often this results in achieving your desired objective.

Don't get me wrong: this will take a consistent effort on your part.

If you've been rude to your spouse for 20 years, you're going to get a funny look when you offer to rub her feet. Stick with it.

Tell your spouse about the depth of your love and that you want your relationship to clearly reflect it. You got married for better or worse. Make it for the better. Envision what the relationship should ideally be for the both of you, and then go out and create it. This process will work effectively in every aspect of your life.

There's a restaurant in Chicago named Ed Debevic's that's famous for the way its servers interact with its customers. They have fun, putting themselves fully into their work. Almost anywhere else in the world they'd be just servers. At this restaurant, they're performers. It's all about perspective.

To be clear, The Sufficiency Theory isn't advocating complacency in any aspect of your life. By no means am I suggesting you sit in a dead-end job or maintain a relationship that isn't working. I am, however, imploring you to implement The Sufficiency Theory before you throw in the towel.

Realigning your perspective doesn't mean denying yourself your objectives. On the contrary, living as if you've already achieved your goals vastly increases your chances of reaching them.

You have the power. Your happiness, or your misery, is yours to control. Put The Sufficiency Theory to work and your life will forever benefit. Just remember:

The destination is the road. The journey is the destination.

Life-Altering Principle #3: The Sufficiency Theory—Takeaways

- Striving for external gratification prevents you from maintaining a feeling of contentment derived from who you are and what you do.

- Stop drawing lines in the sand. Happiness is not a destination that can be reached by attaining select milestones.

- Sufficiency doesn't translate to complacency, nor does it mean denying yourself your objectives.

- Shift your approach from waiting for certain things to happen in order to feel a certain way to feeling and acting that way now. Surprisingly often, this will spur the results you desire to happen.

- It costs you *nothing* to shift from the left side of the board to the right, while not doing so costs you *everything*.

- The destination *is* the road. The *journey* is the destination.

- You are exactly where you're supposed to be.

WHAT IS YOUR *WHAT?*
Case Study #9: Chris Brogan

Chris Brogan is the *NY Times* best-selling author of *The Impact Equation* and *Trust Agents* (cowritten with Julien Smith); CEO of Human Business Works, a publishing and media company that serves the do-it-yourself movement of professional learners; and a sought-after professional keynote speaker. An online enthusiast since 1998, he is frequently published in publications such as *Success, Entrepreneur, USA Today,* and *Forbes* and has appeared on several television shows including Dr. Phil.

Chris started his career in telecom, eventually shifting to wireless, and performed various tasks from customer service and product engineering to project management and designing architectural structure. In 2006, he created the first PodCamp unconference together with Christopher S. Penn and was subsequently hired by Jeff Pulver to run his events.

During this period, Chris realized he could accomplish almost anything (with enough failures) and that collaborating with others was markedly more powerful than attempting to gain traction and notoriety focusing solely on his own causes. To this day, leveraging his partners' talents and abilities, while being helpful and attentive to the needs of others, is a consistent mindset he practices.

Chris is a ***Reinventor*** and his *WHAT* is defined below. Visit www.ChrisBrogan.com for more information.

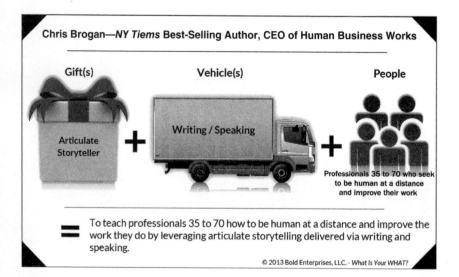

Chris Brogan—NY *Tiems* Best-Selling Author, CEO of Human Business Works

Gift(s)   Vehicle(s)   People

Articulate Storyteller   **+**   Writing / Speaking   **+**   Professionals 35 to 70 who seek to be human at a distance and improve their work

= To teach professionals 35 to 70 how to be human at a distance and improve the work they do by leveraging articulate storytelling delivered via writing and speaking.

© 2013 Bold Enterprises, LLC. - *What Is Your WHAT?*

Life-Altering Principle #4

Retrain Your Brain

The important thing is not to stop questioning.
Curiosity has its own reason for existing.
One cannot help but be in awe when he contemplates the mysteries of eternity,
of life, of the marvelous structure of reality.
It is enough if one tries merely to comprehend a little of this mystery every day.
Never lose a holy curiosity.

—Albert Einstein

As babies, we have wide eyes and are eager to experience the world and learn all we can about it. At some point, though, most of us effectively decide we've learned all we need to know and shut off that wonder-filled openness to the world. It's as if, as adults, we turn off the record button and proceed to live solely on rewind. The result is experiencing life through a filter of preconceived notions that leave little room for profound new discoveries.

But what if you could return to experiencing things for the very first time? How much would you learn if you felt that everyone you encountered had something to teach you?

You can make this happen. You have the ability to *Retrain Your Brain*.

Retrain Your Brain is the principle of experiencing life without the filter of preconceived notions.

Life as a Blank Slate

Imagine Leonardo da Vinci trying to paint the Mona Lisa over his previous classic, *The Last Supper*; or Michael Jackson singing *Thriller* over the track for *Billie Jean*; or Jamie Oliver preparing his best pasta salad on top of an existing salmon dish. The result of each of these attempts would be disastrous. The intent of the artist would be lost amid the chaos of conflicting ideas.

Imagine how less enriched the world would be if our great artists had been unable to spawn new works of art due to their inability to move beyond what they'd already created.

For artists to realize a new vision, they must begin with a blank slate. And the same goes for you.

Your life is being held captive if you deny yourself the ability to create new thoughts and ways of being. When such a repetitive condition exists, growth stops, replaced by a state of complacency.

For example, when you want something to eat, you grab a turkey sandwich because you know you like turkey. When you see your spouse after work, you give each other a peck on the cheek and then review each other's day simply because that's your "Honey, I'm home" interaction. Life is about routine—consistent and predictable. Everything is the way that it's "supposed to be," but you no longer experience the pure joy of being alive.

Try to remember that, at one point, everything was new.

My youngest sons, Isaiah and Xavier, live their lives purely from the state of "I want." It doesn't matter what it is. The boys will play with anything they can get their hands on. Xavier will eat nearly anything we put in front of him. When people come over, Isaiah views them as new friends to play with. For Isaiah and Xavier, life is about trying everything on. Some things fit, others don't. But there's never an internal debate about whether to give something new a whirl.

Throughout childhood and into early adolescence, we're focused on discovery and personal growth. For most people, this learning process stops at some point during adolescence. But if we work at it, we can keep our eyes and minds wide open for our entire lives. When you're able to do so, you have the power to recreate your entire world and smash the rewind button to pieces.

Imagine how different you'd feel if each morning's shower washed away your mental filters and allowed you to take in the day to come as a blank state. Imagine how wondrous each of these situations would feel if approached as if you were experiencing it for the first time:

- Taking on a work assignment
- Walking in your neighborhood
- Playing with your kids
- Enjoying *happy time* with your spouse
- Talking to a stranger
- Eating food
- Drinking wine
- Exercising
- Coming home from work

Can you imagine how different speaking with a loved one would be if you put aside the memory of thousands of previous conversations and fully paid attention to how the two of you were interacting? Instead of being rote and repetitive, it would be an exchange of true communication and revelation.

It's also important that you break past the "personal language" you've created for yourself. When someone says X to you, you translate it to mean Y. When you encounter an event that's in some ways similar to Z, you simply categorize it as Z—missing subtleties that could yield deeper understanding. The language you've developed is uniquely yours, but if it's all you speak, you'll never learn other people's languages. And if you rely only on what you know to assign meanings, you cut off the opportunity to see the world from different perspectives. Consider William Shakespeare's famous line from *Hamlet*:

"*There is nothing either good or bad, but thinking makes it so.*"

For example, you may look at a tree and see life. However, the person next to you might view it as shade; and the person across the street might perceive it as an overgrown weed. Your life directly reflects the colored glasses you're wearing. Consider trying on a new pair of specs.

Of course, there's much to be said for experience. Learning from your past is one of the points of being human. This isn't about wiping your memory clean. It's about not letting what you know blind you to learning even more. The goal is to achieve life as a blank slate as your default way of being.

Free Yourself of Generalizations

A critical step in learning to Retrain Your Brain is to clear away the muddle of generalizations. Lazy phrases such as "that's not me," "that's just how things are," or "people are like that" are too often used as easy excuses to avoid the unfamiliar. Becoming keenly aware of how often generalizations influence your thinking—and evasion of thinking—is an important step toward achieving positive, permanent change.

An integral part of this process is questioning your automatic responses. For instance, if you've never eaten Ethiopian food because you believe you wouldn't like it, question why. If you don't have a good reason, then the next time you see an Ethiopian restaurant, stop in and pick something up (I highly recommend the doro tibs wat). If you decide it's not your bag, you're out $10, but you gave it a go. Then again, you may discover it's your new favorite meal.

As a more extreme example, some dismiss an entire subset of humanity due to bigotry: "I don't socialize with that type" or "those people are nothing but trouble." This type of prejudice isn't learned from experience, but passed down from generation to generation due to ignorance. Holding onto such generalizations does nothing but cripple your ability to fully experience other people . . . and your own life.

Rid yourself of generalizations to open yourself up to options.

In 2008 my family had a birthday party for my son Xavier, who was turning two, at a terrific place called Pump It Up. It's a facility filled with huge inflatable play areas and a climbing wall. All the kids had a blast jumping around, going through the mazes, and climbing the wall. My wife and I had never been on a climbing wall, so we both decided to give it a try. It was a fun diversion, especially reaching the top and rappelling down.

A few minutes later, I looked around and was shocked to see my 66-year-old mother wearing the harness and climbing the wall! It would've been easy for her to say, "I've never done this before, and I'm 66 years old, so forget it." But she didn't let a lazy generalization about giving up on new experiences past a certain age keep her from fully living. In a few minutes, she was halfway up the wall. She didn't make it all the way to the top (because she had on business attire and dress shoes), but she broke down a lot of barriers with that climb.

Too often, people fail to try something new. Or they may give it a quick try but give up after encountering the first sign of difficulty. Don't be one of those people. Legend has it that Colonel Sanders had his chicken recipe rejected more than 1,000 times by restaurant owners before he found a partner willing to back him. If he'd simply said, "I guess I'm just not a cook," think of all the jobs that would never have been created and the millions of customers who would never have enjoyed his chicken.

Close the gap between living in a state of wonder and being dissuaded by the generalizations you've unconsciously put in place to limit your thoughts and your willingness to take on the unfamiliar. Ultimately, your life's true power is in the pencil, not the eraser.

Compression = Depression

As we get older, we tend to compress the details of experiences into a finite set of categories. When we encounter a new experience, we slap one of our existing labels onto it—whether or not it's a good match. While it's convenient to instantly identify anything we come across with as something familiar, it can be terribly limiting; it dampens our ability to see things clearly, make exciting discoveries, and grow. Further, it creates a distorted perspective of the past, which can lead to inappropriate behavior in the present.

For example, pretend for a moment that you were continually praised as a child regardless of what you did. Your compression of those encounters leads you to believe that you can do no wrong. The result is you have problems accepting responsibility for the times when you screw up. Further, when someone is legitimately angry with you because of a mistake you made, you don't really hear what's being said because your reaction can't get beyond, "I'm perfect. What's this guy's problem?" This self-assurance soothes you, but people grow tired of your being out of touch with the world and stop trying to establish meaningful relationships with you.

Conversely, pretend for a minute that you were continually blamed as a child and told you were bad. Your compression of those encounters leads you to believe that you can do nothing right. The result is your feeling awful about yourself no matter how much people like and respect you. You react with suspicion when people praise you and ruin the chances of reaching your potential.

Pay attention to how you internalize and compress your life experiences.

Although this may be painful to hear, a lot of the assumptions you live with every day are built on inaccuracies. As long as you refuse to face reality, you won't be able to distinguish truth from fantasy. So take the time to examine the memories that filter how you experience the world.

Equally important, move the processing of your experiences away from compression and categorization. Compression leads to depression. Try to treat each event as its own experience.

The Gift of Your Pre-Sent Future

In recent years, virtually every self-help doctrine has strongly championed *living in the moment* to reach your full potential. But that phrase carries a number of different meanings. In this book, *living in the moment* means not allowing past experiences to blind you to what's happening *right now*.

In part, that means paying full attention. But it also means letting go of anything from the past that isn't helpful to you. If you have a personal video you play over and over in your head, edit that tape to cut out anything that limits you. Or just turn off the video altogether.

> *Anything from your past that you choose to relive becomes a part of your identity. Be careful about which memories you commit to.*

Every limiting thought hinders the creation of an unfiltered way of being. Think about this the next time you choose to expend energy on something that happened an hour ago, let alone 10 years ago. It's common for people to insert instances from their past into their current experiences, continuously reliving events they believe shape who they are. But if you refuse to give it power, the past will have no impact on what you do with the brand new moment that stands before you.

As for the future, it represents the great unknown. While we sometimes like to believe that we can predict what will happen, the future has its own special plans and frequently does the opposite of what was expected. Many fear the future, but that makes as little sense as living in the past. You can't control either.

And, while *living in the moment* is desirable, even with the speed of The Flash, it's nearly impossible to do because life happens by the millisecond.

I propose there's a fourth moment in time over which you *do* have control, however. Harbhajan Singh Khalsa Yogiji, a.k.a. Yogi Bhajan, former spiritual director of the 3HO Foundation, refers to this point in time as your *Pre-Sent Future*.

To understand the Pre-Sent Future, picture a treadmill (see Figure 10.1). At the back of the treadmill's belt, behind where you're running, is your past. At the front of the treadmill's belt, ahead of where you're running, is your future. The spot where you foot lands is your present.

Living within your Pre-Sent Future requires that you continually load the front of the treadmill's belt with exactly what you want. Your feelings, desires, dreams, and objectives—pile them all up in front of you, perhaps forming a brick wall.

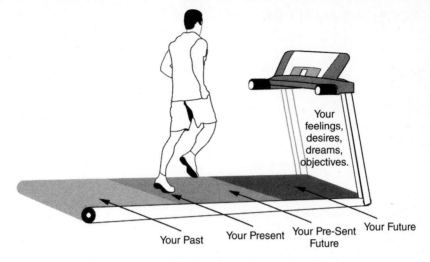

Figure 10.1   The Pre-Sent Future Treadmill

As the belt of the treadmill revolves, a small piece of the wall breaks off and lands directly in your present. Your next step will be met with another goal you've laid out in front of you, and so on.

As long as the future is filled with what you desire and create, as the past loops under the deck and makes its way towards you in an attempt to become a part of your present, it will be blocked by all of your future objectives and hold no power.

> **The Pre-Sent Future is about being in charge of, and creating,
> the next moment in your life.**

For example, if you covet calm and peace, establish a mind-set of calm and peace while anticipating anything that might disrupt it, and act accordingly. As spiritual guru Iyanla Vanzant put it, "If you see crazy coming, cross the street." As another example, if you have a huge project due in a week, split it into manageable pieces and get started right away. Don't wait until 24 hours before it's due to begin.

Living within your Pre-Sent eliminates much of life's randomness because it enables you to create the life you most desire by maintaining a sniper-like focus. If you clearly establish what you want your future to look like and load your Pre-Sent Future with your desired objectives, you'll operate from a foundation of clarity and strength.

Otherwise, there's only one thing you'll have coming to you—your persistent past.

The Voice of Conjecture

A key element of Retrain Your Brain is to understand the Voice of Conjecture and how it rules your life. The dictionary definition of conjecture is "inference or judgment based on inconclusive or incomplete evidence; a statement, opinion, or conclusion based on guesswork."

This describes how most people live. We're swift to form opinions and seldom allow the time to gather all available evidence before setting our decisions in stone.

Think back on your life. How often have you assumed someone acted out of malice only to discover the person meant no harm at all? How many times have you sworn off a friend only to have that person end up being one of your closest confidants? How frequently do you make a decision you later regret?

To move toward life as a blank slate, train yourself to gather enough information to make decisions based on facts, not speculation. The impulse that encourages you to make rapid decisions is what I call the Voice of Conjecture. It leads you to stick with what you know, and avoid learning and growing. The more you give in to it, the less control you have over the quality of your life.

The first step towards freedom is moving the Voice of Conjecture from your unconscious to your conscious mind. This allows you to recognize when it's attempting to impose shortcuts on a rational decision-making process. Once you become aware of the Voice of Conjecture, tell it to wait while you find out what you need to know to make the best choice. Otherwise, if you keep operating as you always have, you'll realize the same inevitable results.

It's unrealistic to expect the Voice of Conjecture to disappear entirely. It's been a part of you for so long that it's tenured in its current position. However, you can work to loosen its hold on you, one notch at a time. The more you do so, the greater the benefits you'll reap from interacting with life as it happens.

Your Very Own Crystal Ball

Finally, I want you to think about events in your life that you were hesitant, or even refused, to take on because you couldn't possibly know the outcome. Whether it was a confrontation with a friend, riding the new Dive of Death roller coaster, embarking on a new career, or telling someone "I love you," reflect on as many of these YāNo moments as you can.

Most people will choose what's most familiar over embarking on a journey where the potential rewards are great but the outcome is uncertain. Is that what you did?

You hold in your hands your very own crystal ball—because if fear keeps you from pursuing what's unfamiliar and uncomfortable, it's easy to predict your future. It'll be exactly like your past.

Your crystal ball shows that you'll be alive in the future. But will you be truly living?

If you're comfortable where you are and don't feel the need for challenges, why consider a different path? After all, you're not hurting anyone, are you? The honest answer is *yes*. You're hurting yourself. And you're denying the rest of us the possibility of benefiting from your contributions. You've given up on life and you don't even realize it.

Retrain Your Brain to let go of the past, make new discoveries, and open yourself up to fully experience all the universe has to offer. You have extraordinary contributions to make and an incredible life to share. But you must be willing to quiet the Voice of Conjecture and take on what makes you most *uncomfortable*.

Being afraid of the unknown is perfectly normal, but sticking exclusively with what you know is a death sentence.

What will your future hold?

Life-Altering Principle #4: Retrain Your Brain—Takeaways

- Experience life as a blank slate without the filter of preconceived notions.
- Everyone you encounter has something to teach you.
- At one point, everything was new.
- Reawaken childlike discovery within you.
- Move past your own personal language.
- Compression leads to depression. Try to treat each event as its own experience.
- Don't let what you know blind you to learning even more.
- Remember Shakespeare's observation that "There is nothing either good or bad, but thinking makes it so."
- Anything from your past that you choose to relive becomes a part of your identity. Be careful about which memories you commit to.
- Rid yourself of generalizations and you'll open yourself up to options.
- Take control of your Pre-Sent Future.
- Follow Iyanla Vanzant's advice: "If you see crazy coming, cross the street."
- Keep your past exactly where it belongs.
- Quiet the Voice of Conjecture.
- Embark on journeys where the outcome is uncertain but the rewards are potentially great.

WHAT IS YOUR *WHAT?*
Case Study #10: Ron White

Ron White is the 2009 and 2010 U.S.A. Memory Champion, former U.S. record holder for memorizing a deck of cards in 87 seconds, and military veteran who served in Afghanistan. Since the age of 18, he has taught people how to improve their memory so they can make more money, stop losing business, and massively increase productivity.

A college dropout, Ron began his career as a telemarketer for The Memory Institute, securing speaking gigs for the company's trainers. After taking the course, he shifted to presenting, becoming the company's youngest speaker and one of its best. Before long, he started his own venture and has been an in-demand corporate trainer and entertainer ever since.

A media veteran who has appeared extensively on television including Martha Stewart, where he memorized every page of her magazine, Ron's unique style and innate abilities have helped him gain national recognition. Recently, he embarked on a countrywide tour with a 7' x 50' portable wall and, from memory, writes the rank, first name, and last name of all 2,000 soldiers who died serving in Afghanistan. The theme of the mission is "You Are Not Forgotten."

Ron is a **Birther** and his *WHAT* is defined below. Visit BrainAthlete.com or RonWhiteTraining.com for more information.

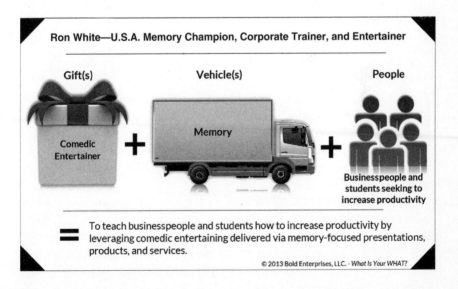

Ron White—U.S.A. Memory Champion, Corporate Trainer, and Entertainer

Gift(s)	Vehicle(s)	People
Comedic Entertainer	Memory	Businesspeople and students seeking to increase productivity

= To teach businesspeople and students how to increase productivity by leveraging comedic entertaining delivered via memory-focused presentations, products, and services.

© 2013 Bold Enterprises, LLC. - *What Is Your WHAT?*

Life-Altering Principle #5

The Altar of Jack's Cathedral

Control your own destiny or someone else will.

—Jack Welch

Jack Welch, the chairman and CEO of General Electric from 1981 to 2001, is renowned for creating a world-class organization through his disciplined approach to management, intuitive decision-making, and ability to bring out the absolute best in his team. His innovative business ideas took GE from a market worth of $14 billion in 1981 to $410 billion in 2001, making it the most valuable company in the world.

Many of Welch's concepts for running a successful business can have an equally profound impact when applied to your personal choices. After all, you're the CEO of your life; think of it as *You, Inc.*

To achieve success in all aspects of your life, run it like a Fortune 500 company. For example, have an operational plan that drives your key decisions, day-to-day interactions, and selection of team members. Without a clear focus on goals, you'll make poor decisions that lead to frustration and unhappiness.

Like a corporation, you're split into divisions. You have a personal life, which includes friends and family. You have a business life, which generates your income. You have a leisure life, which includes your hobbies. And you have a spiritual life, which keeps you centered. Each division has its own set of operating procedures.

A key reason for Jack Welch's success was his ability to keep each corporate division focused on his overall vision for the organization while encouraging autonomy. You should manage your life in a similar way.

You can do so by incorporating many of Welch's best practices into your personal life—that is, stand on *The Altar of Jack's Cathedral.*

The Altar of Jack's Cathedral is the principle of incorporating Jack Welch's successful business practices into your personal behavior. The result is achieving maximum effectiveness in all areas of your life.

Clearly Identify Your Vision and Make It Known

Jack Welch wore his vision on his sleeve. From day one of taking over GE, Welch articulated an easily understood plan for where he wanted to take the company. Soon there wasn't an employee, stockholder, or corporate partner who wasn't crystal clear about Welch's ideas for moving GE forward. Though Welch often adjusted his views to fit changing circumstances, he was relentless in sharing his current vision with everyone. This created an exceptionally strong corporate culture.

There was little confusion among GE's nearly 450,000 employees and hundreds of companies around the world as to Welch's overriding philosophy for GE. From the executive level to a brand new hire, choices were made that adhered to Welch's widely disseminated processes for achievement. The key to business success is to empower those with whom you work to make choices within the parameters of transparent guidelines. Without a well-structured declaration of operational procedures, any choice can be made, and the odds are it will be to the detriment of the company.

Welch worked hard to create a distinct corporate culture for GE and left no room for uncertainty. If a company wanted to do business with GE, it would have to be within a pre-defined set of expectations. Employees across all business divisions of GE needed to be unified by a defined goal, a single overriding purpose to achieve global success. And guess what? The same concept applies to you and your life. The key is to become highly focused on who you are, what your purpose is, and what you stand for. You can do this by defining your own internal culture and being consistent in your approach to all areas of your life.

There's great value to be gained in following Welch's example of wearing your vision on your sleeve and behaving in ways that exemplify your vision. Whether you're spending time with friends and family, working, playing games, or praying with others of your faith, who you are and how you interact with others will be unwavering, and most importantly, consistent with your true self.

The Vitality Curve

One of Jack Welch's biggest challenges was maintaining a high degree of team member excellence while developing a system for personnel development that fostered differentiation and potential. With hundreds of thousands of employees and hundreds of companies spread throughout the world, it was important for GE to develop a sustainable system to evaluate the aptitude of its top executives. GE was too large for Welch and his executive team to be involved with each of its companies on a day-to-day basis. Therefore, GE's success required hiring, and maintaining, the highest grade of talent available for each company and allowing each unit to operate semi-independently.

To sustain its competitive edge and avoid an unfocused, monolithic culture, Welch and his team created an evaluation matrix called The Vitality Curve. It required the executives within each business unit to rank its managers into a Top 20 Percent, Vital 70 Percent, or Bottom 10 Percent. The underperformers in the Bottom 10 Percent generally had to go.

In Welch's book *Jack: Straight from the Gut*, he wrote, "Making these judgments is not easy, nor always precise. Year after year, differentiation raises the bar and increases the overall caliber of the organization. It's a dynamic process, and no one is assured of staying in the top group forever. They have to constantly demonstrate they deserve to be there."

This is an incredibly powerful concept that you can immediately apply. Think about the four key areas of your life:

1. Family and friends
2. Work
3. Hobbies
4. Spirituality

To help drive home the importance of this concept, I want you to create your own Vitality Curve using Figure 11.1. Alternatively, you can download the template at www.WhatIsYourWhat.com/resources and print as many copies as you like.

The Vitality Curve				
	Family and Friends	9 to 5	Hobbies/ Avocation	Spiritual
T o p 2 0				
V i t a l 7 0				
B o t t o m 1 0				

Figure 11.1   The Vitality Curve Template

To begin, take a few minutes to think about the top section. When you're ready, write in the top third of the page and the pertinent quadrants of your Top 20 Percent:

- The family members and friends you love most
- The most fulfilling tasks associated with your job
- The hobbies that give you the most joy
- The spiritual endeavors that bring you the most peace and contentment

It is this 20 percent that brings you 90 percent or more of what you find most fulfilling in life. Take a few minutes to think about the next section. When you're ready, fill in the middle third of the page and the pertinent quadrants of your vital 70 percent:

- The family members and friends you moderately enjoy
- The tasks for your job that are merely tolerable
- The hobbies you maintain but don't really thrill you
- The elements of your spiritual endeavors that aren't entirely satisfying

This vital 70 percent represents aspects of your life that aren't sources of great joy but that you can accept as necessary or "good enough."

Finally, take a few moments to think about the last section. When you're ready, fill in the pertinent quadrants for your bottom 10 percent:

- The family members and friends who cause you grief
- The tasks for your job that you abhor
- The hobbies you stopped truly enjoying years ago
- The spiritual endeavors that bring you significant discontent

This bottom 10 percent represents the aspects of your life that cause most of your stress and unhappiness.

When you're finished, please review the entire Vitality Curve and double-check that you've included each person, activity, or interaction that should be listed. This powerful exercise will help you understand what drives you on a daily basis, as well as the impact that various people and activities have on your life.

You're now ready to act on your new understanding. The next three sections teach you how.

Make a Plan to Address Your Bottom 10 Percent

Wayne W. Dyer wrote in his 1992 book *Real Magic: Creating Miracles in Everyday Life*, "There are no accidents in life. Each experience we have, no matter how painful, eventually leads us to something of higher value."

A common knee-jerk reaction is to get rid of the Bottom 10 Percent immediately. Before you do so, however, ask yourself what life lessons you're receiving from these people and activities. While it may eventually prove necessary to eliminate the aspects of your life that drag you down, first take care to consider why the Bottom 10 Percent is part of your world. Understanding what you loathe, and why, can help you better appreciate what you most value and love.

It's also possible that what you loathe hits too close to home. Think about this before making any rash decisions. Keep in mind that when you point one finger out, you've got three pointing right back at you.

That said, if permanently removing these people and activities from your life will vastly improve it, then it's time to do so . . . with no excuses.

You might protest: "How can I dismiss someone from my life if I have to see him at every family holiday?" There are always options. For example, you can choose to skip attending the family holidays that include this relative and create other occasions to be with the rest of your family. Or you can request that this family member not be invited to events you attend.

Another option is to handle the situation like Jane M., an associate of mine from Cleveland, Ohio. Though she loves her family's get-togethers, a verbally abusive relationship with her brother often affects her ability to enjoy them. Recently she initiated a new plan of action. When her brother says something rude or ignorant—which always happens—she simply takes a deep breath, looks him in the eye, and says "Okay, whatever you say."

This easy-to-implement and empowering approach takes the victory out of his insults by making it clear they no longer diminish her, allowing Jane to continue taking part in an annual event she cherishes.

As another example, maybe there's an activity at work you've become expert at but loathe with every fiber of your being. If no one else is qualified to take it over, how can you give it up? One answer is to simply train a colleague to take your place or swap activities. If you play your cards right, you may choose someone who actually enjoys the activity, and you'll have not only lightened your burden but made a coworker happy.

Making these decisions is not always easy. But as Jack Welch said, more often than not your life will be the better for making tough choices.

Examine What You've Listed Under Your Vital 70 Percent

Over the next two to three months, take a hard look at the people and activities falling into this category. Either improve upon your Vital 70 Percent so you're able to move some people and activities into the Top 20 Percent for your next Vitality Curve, or relegate some people and activities into your Bottom 10 Percent and choose how to deal with them.

Consider Your Top 20 Percent

Quite simply, these people and activities should be the focus of your life. Your Top 20 Percent accounts for the lion's share of your fulfillment and joy, and deserves the majority of your attention. Think about the satisfaction you'll experience from concentrating on your Top 20 Percent . . . and do it.

Leveraging the Vitality Curve will enable you to establish a highly focused approach to living. I encourage you to create a new Vitality Curve every 6 to 12 months. This will provide you with clear priorities, help motivate you to cut out whatever drags you down, and spend more time with the people and activities truly important to you.

Six Sigma

One of Jack Welch's smartest moves was being among the first to implement a set of practices called Six Sigma. The initiative was created in 1986 by Bill Smith, a senior scientist at Motorola, to improve manufacturing processes and eliminate defects. The concept was so successful that it was extended to other types of business processes, with *defect* being defined as anything that could lead to customer dissatisfaction.

The objective is to eliminate virtually all possibility for customer discontent. A typical business might tolerate achieving a standard of Three Sigma, which is 66,800 DPMO (defective parts per million opportunities), a 93.32 percent efficiency; or Four Sigma, which is 6,210 DPMO, a 99.379 percent efficiency. But a company that achieves Six Sigma standards will tolerate no more than 3.4 DPMO, or 99.9997 percent efficiency. This may seem like an overbearing commitment to quality. However, a company the size of GE manufactures tens of millions of parts, so even a small defect rate can have significant financial repercussions.

The same idea applies to achieving total customer satisfaction. Even one negative impression made on a customer could result in the loss of millions of dollars of revenue to GE over the lifetime of that failed relationship.

Think about the four key areas of your life, and the effect that maintaining Six Sigma quality would have on each of them:

- **Family and Friends:** Do you spend enough time with family and friends, or are you away at work focusing on projects that you don't even care about? When you're with your family and friends, are you really there, or do you miss important details because your TV, smartphone, or thoughts distract you? When you participate in activities with family and friends, do you commit 100 percent to them? Are you fully open and authentic with your loved ones?

- **Work:** When you're at work, do you address your responsibilities with 100 percent commitment? Do you proactively take steps to improve the practices being used? Do you treat your coworkers with kindness and consideration? Or are you there to simply collect a paycheck?

- **Hobbies:** If you participate in sports, do you plunge into each game with total commitment? If you play cards, are you concentrating on every nuance occurring at the table? If you're an amateur artist, do you put your heart and soul into each piece you create? Are you working toward turning your beloved hobby into a career? Are you leaving no stone unturned in pursuit of perfecting your craft?

- **Spirituality:** When you worship, are you fully committed? Are you actively seeking to connect with a higher power? Are you open to receiving answers to your prayers? Do you always keep an eye out for hints, subtle (and not so subtle) messages, and coincidences? Do you work at helping others? Do you contribute toward helping your place of worship attain its objectives?

Your goal is to achieve Six Sigma in all key aspects of your life. This is highly challenging but achievable. It requires committing to the people and activities you care most about with your heart and soul, fully participating in all critical areas of your life, and maintaining high standards for everything you pursue.

No one can be perfect all the time; but you can strive to accept nothing less than your best. Realizing that you're not giving something your all, and adjusting your attitude and behavior to full commitment, is the first step to embedding the Six Sigma concept into who you are.

By focusing your time and energy on the people and activities that most directly support your becoming your true self, you vastly increase your chances of winning at this game called life.

Boundaryless Behavior

The last Jack Welch idea I'll share is what he called *Boundaryless Behavior*. He defined this as "the creation of a boundaryless company where all functions—engineering, manufacturing, marketing, and the rest—would operate within an operational environment that did not have barriers between the units." Today, this may sound like common practice. But at the time, in late 1989, this was revolutionary. Large, bureaucratic corporations simply did not operate in this manner.

It took several years to implement, but the result of this initiative was the unbridled sharing of information and personnel between the units—and an especially prosperous period for GE. Applying this approach to your life can reap similar rewards.

> *How often do you get tied up in Emotional Bureaucracy? Is making a decision for you a decision-making process in itself?*

Many of us get so weighed down in deciding whether to pursue an opportunity that the opportunity either disappears or is taken advantage of by someone else. This ranges from failing to act on a business innovation to letting the girl or boy of your dreams slip away.

For example, when you come up with a novel approach to making something better, or are struck like a bolt of lightning by a revolutionary idea, the universe is giving you a chance to have an extraordinary impact. Have you ever been blessed with such an inspiration and then sat on it?

Like a burning desire that won't be smoldered until it's satisfied, such an opportunity will continue to seek someone ready to fully receive it and bring it to fruition. Remember how you felt when, a few years after your brainstorm (e.g., a blanket with sleeves), you watched someone else reap the wealth and fame of delivering your idea to the world?

The sinking feeling that you got in the pit of your stomach was your soul kicking you as hard as it could. It's vital to be ready to receive and act upon such opportunities whenever they occur.

The first step is to learn to accurately share information between the various divisions of You, Inc. Let your altruism talk to your greed. Let your happiness have a meeting with your self-destructiveness. Set up a closed-door session for your fear to hammer it out with your hope. Get the various aspects of who you are freely communicating with each other to eliminate decision bottlenecks. Allow all your top decision-making divisions access to the same data.

You may find it necessary to do some reorganization—for example, firing fear from his post as chairman of the board and replacing it with a clearly defined set of objectives.

When you're done, your Emotional Bureaucracy should no longer be a barrier to making decisions; you should be able to recognize and respond to opportunities swiftly and confidently.

Of course, taking greater risks means you're also likely to make a greater number of errors. That's okay. You'll learn and grow, much more from making mistakes than from taking no action at all.

> **When looking back on your life, you'll regret failing to act much more than taking action and experiencing so-called "failure."**

A failed attempt at bringing something to fruition does not translate to being a failure. Failure is often a word of ignorance people choose to throw out at those who dare to soar in an attempt to bring them down.

There are myriad ways to internalize life's experiences and the words you encounter. Failure is a highly charged word and carries implicit connotations . . . or does it? Take a moment to write the word *failure* and how you define it on the lines below:

_____

_____

_____

Most people associate the word with one's inability to accomplish a set task. Did you? If so, consider that alternatives exist. The word's effect is only as powerful and life-altering as the power you grant it. I choose to view failure as "success, with an unintended ending." Do you like that definition better?

The quality of your life is directly proportional to your positive or negative internal dialogue and your willingness to act upon opportunity when it knocks. Ignoring it is a sure-fire formula for mediocrity. Commit to internal Boundaryless Behavior and become comfortable acting quickly and decisively.

More Wisdom from Jack Welch

This chapter has covered just a few of the highlights to be found in Jack Welch's *Jack: Straight from the Gut*. I encourage you to read what is one of the most profoundly helpful business books ever written.

Life-Altering Principle #5: The Altar of Jack's Cathedral—Takeaways

- Achieve maximum effectiveness in all areas of your life by incorporating Jack Welch's successful business practices into your behavior.
- You're the CEO of your life. Think of it as *You, Inc.* and operate like a Fortune 500 company.
- Become highly focused on who you are, what you stand for, and what your purpose is.
- Leave no room for uncertainty. Wear your vision on your sleeve.
- Identify the Top 20 Percent, Vital 70 Percent, and Bottom 10 Percent for each area of your life.
- Commit to the people and activities you care about most, fully participate in all critical areas of your life, and maintain high standards for everything you pursue.
- Eliminate Emotional Bureaucracy.
- Keep in mind that when looking back on your life, you'll regret failing to act much more than taking action.
- View failure as "success, with an unintended ending."

WHAT IS YOUR *WHAT?*
Case Study #11: Dan Miller

Dan Miller is the President of 48 Days, LLC, best-selling author of *48 Days To The Work You Love*, and a frequent media guest who has appeared on CBS' *The Early Show*, MSNBC's *Hard Ball with Chris Matthews*, and Dave Ramsey's nationally syndicated radio show. An in-demand speaker and popular podcaster, Dan's work focuses on helping people integrate their dreams and passions into daily activities.

A psychology major in college, he subscribed to Jung's theory that, in order to be an effective therapist, one must have significant life experience and attain meaningful intellectual capital. This philosophy led to his pursuit of various endeavors, including selling used cars, owning health clubs, university teaching, and sales training. At the age of 45, and as a result of being consistently asked for career and life advice, Dan introduced a Sunday school course at his church named *Career Life Transitions* to help parishioners discover, and realize, the work they are driven to pursue.

The course was an immediate hit and Dan proceeded to create an easy-to-follow curriculum based on his teachings. After selling nearly $2,000,000 in product both in-person and online, he was approached with myriad expansion opportunities. Today, Dan leads an active community of game changers who are committed to finding—or creating—work that is meaningful, purposeful, and profitable . . . in 48 days.

Dan is a **Shifter** and his *WHAT* is defined below. Visit 48Days.com and 48Days.net for more information.

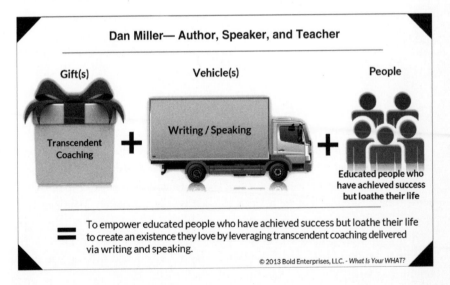

Dan Miller— Author, Speaker, and Teacher

Gift(s) + Vehicle(s) + People

Transcendent Coaching + Writing / Speaking + Educated people who have achieved success but loathe their life

= To empower educated people who have achieved success but loathe their life to create an existence they love by leveraging transcendent coaching delivered via writing and speaking.

© 2013 Bold Enterprises, LLC. - *What Is Your WHAT?*

Life-Altering Principle #6

The Not-So-Golden Rule

Love many things, for therein lies the true strength, and whosoever loves much performs much, and can achieve much, and what is done in love is done well.

—Vincent van Gogh

Throughout your life, you've probably been told to live by the Golden Rule: *Do unto others as you would have others do unto you.* Variations of this include *What goes around comes around* and *As you treat others, so shall you be treated.* Some refer to this circular motion of energy as "karma."

The idea is that by releasing positive thoughts and actions into the universe, something positive will come back to you. Conversely, if you emanate negative thoughts and actions, you can expect to encounter something ugly down the road.

The problem with these concepts is that they're built on an unstable foundation of guilt and fear. They're societal constructs designed to keep you from harming others.

While that's a laudable goal, you have to be careful not to be so focused on doing "the right thing" that you harm yourself. Too often we make choices based on guilt or fear of retribution rather than on what's truly right for us. In this chapter, I propose an alternative way of thinking that will serve you more effectively.

> *The Not-So-Golden Rule is the principle of eliminating fear*
> *or expectation as a motive for your actions.*

Motive Does Matter

Consider the Golden Rule and karma for a moment, and think about what they have in common. To my mind, the most important overlap is that they both promote behavior driven by expectation.

This is self-evident with karma. But even the *Do unto others as you would have others do unto you* message essentially promises that if you're good to people, you can expect them to be good to you in turn. It's an implied social contract.

However, the real world is more complicated than that. Some people read your being nice to them as an invitation to treat you shabbily; and some insist on your treating them poorly before they'll respect you. Then again, some people have an agenda so unwavering that how you treat them will have no effect whatsoever on their behavior.

There's nothing wrong with the overt messages: *Do good.* You absolutely should do good. But you shouldn't do so expecting a quid pro quo.

You may want to believe your positive actions will pave the road for you with blessings, but think about it. When a child is killed by gang crossfire, did she somehow deserve her fate because she was a colicky baby? What about the adult who commits heinous crimes and yet is never convicted; do you believe that as a boy he walked hundreds of old ladies across the street and earned his "Get Out of Jail Free" card?

While there are examples of someone receiving a large inheritance after dedicating her life to public service, there are also examples of kind, loving people dying alone after years of living in squalor.

There is often little correlation between good intentions and rewards, yet many of us hold the misguided notion that one can create "good" or "bad" karma based on daily activities.

Actually, Hinduism defines karma as "the totality of actions and their concomitant reactions in this and previous lives, all of which determines our future." In other words, current positive or negative actions are only elements of a bigger picture that includes what's happened in your past.

Your impetus for taking action should reflect your simply wanting to do so. Only when you remove the expectation for reward, or what the Hindu call *Vedas* (reaping what you sow), will you realize the true benefit of serving others. As Tony Robbins says, "Motive does matter."

While it's admirable to give more than you expect to receive, giving more than you believe you're able to give manifests long-term contentment.

Begin questioning your motives. What is it that you expect to receive in return for your efforts?

The point of *The Not-So-Golden Rule* is to eliminate all ties to expectation. This will allow your motive for action to shift from anticipating a certain response to acting simply because you choose to. Once you can get to the point of expecting nothing in return for your actions, you'll be in a position to receive everything.

Let Love Rule

For years I tuned into Dr. Laura Schlessinger's radio show. At first I found her brash, often insensitive, and sometimes just mean. After listening to her for a while, however, I began to understand that while her on-air persona takes a no-nonsense, no-holds-barred approach with callers, her method of counseling is built on a foundation of love.

Schlessinger has an uncanny ability to know when a caller needs a swift kick in the rear. Her tough-love tactics are never meant to deliver pain but to free callers from whatever emotional muck they're stuck in, and move them onward and upward. Dr. Laura has identified her framework for living clearly. Her counseling is consistent. Her style is unwavering.

Though some who call don't receive the answers they were hoping to hear, her advice is always in line with her principles. Countless times over the years, I've heard someone who fought Dr. Laura over her advice call back a few weeks later to say that the suggestions really worked.

What amazes me most about Dr. Laura is how much she really does care about each and every caller. There are those she can't help because they just don't want to be helped, but the vast majority of the time a caller leaves with a new perspective and new positive attitude.

It's because of her commitment to love, without the expectation of reciprocation, that Dr. Laura was able to build one of the biggest brands in all of radio.

One of Dr. Laura's overriding principles is being the person to whom you want to come home. If you're married, pamper your spouse. Say sweet nothings. Bring breakfast to bed. Make your home an oasis.

That may sound similar to the Golden Rule or karma. The key difference is to act out of love, without the expectation of *anything* in return. You love because

Figure 12.1 My Forearm Tattoo—Worth Every Second of Pain Endured

you want to, not because you need that person to love you back. Of course, the latter might happen. But there's a big difference between saying "I love you" because you want to be loved and saying it simply because you want to express how you feel.

It's possible to find love in everything you do. Whether at work, with family and friends, in your hobbies, or at your place of worship, look for love and act on it. Period.

In the words of my favorite musician, Lenny Kravitz, and the words tattooed on my forearm: "Let Love Rule" (see Figure 12.1). It's within this pure state of effortless bliss that you'll find peace and contentment.

By establishing love as the ruler of your domain, and taking action without expectation of reward, you'll realize spiritual wealth of far greater value than gold.

Life-Altering Principle #6: The Not-So-Golden Rule—Takeaways

- Expect nothing from your actions. You may find that when you're in this mind-set, you'll receive everything.
- Eliminate the perceived correlation between your actions and the results realized.
- Establish love as the ruler of your domain.
- Motive does matter. Question yours.
- Find love in everything you do.
- It's in a state of pure, effortless bliss where you'll find peace and contentment.
- Give much more than you believe you are able to give.

WHAT IS YOUR *WHAT?*
Case Study #12: Mari Smith

Mari Smith is the author of *The New Relationship Marketing* and a leading social media strategist who is widely recognized as the premier Facebook marketing expert in the world. A technology veteran and keynote speaker, she was named one of the top ten Social Media Influencers by *Forbes* and frequently shares the stage with notable leaders and celebrities, including Sir Richard Branson, the Dalai Lama, and Tony Robbins.

She began her career in Scotland as an administrative assistant, eventually shifting to sales and marketing positions. In 1999, she moved to California and immersed herself in the fields of relationships, marketing, and Internet technology. In 2007, Mari was invited to join a Facebook app beta team and social media immediately became her focus.

Today, she has ~800,000 social media connections and her company provides in-depth training to entrepreneurs and corporations. Mari is a frequent media guest and has been featured in publications such as the *NY Times,* the *Wall Street Journal, Inc., Fortune,* the *Chicago Tribune,* and *Success.*

Mari is a **Shifter** and her *WHAT* is defined below. Visit MariSmith.com for more information.

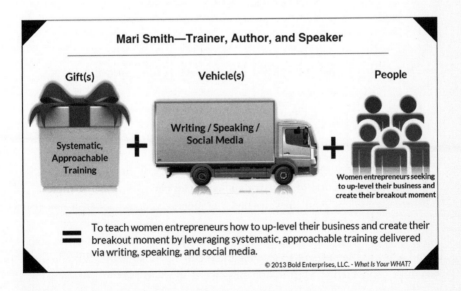

Mari Smith—Trainer, Author, and Speaker

Gift(s) + Vehicle(s) + People

Systematic, Approachable Training

Writing / Speaking / Social Media

Women entrepreneurs seeking to up-level their business and create their breakout moment

= To teach women entrepreneurs how to up-level their business and create their breakout moment by leveraging systematic, approachable training delivered via writing, speaking, and social media.

© 2013 Bold Enterprises, LLC. - *What Is Your WHAT?*

Life-Altering Principle #7

The Slow Death of Not Being the Star

The critic has to educate the public. The artist has to educate the critic.

—Oscar Wilde

Tens of millions of people know who the celebrity of the moment is dating. But only a fraction of that vast audience can plainly state what they want for themselves. And an even smaller number have a six-month or one-year plan for reaching their goals.

Why are so many driven to live vicariously through others? Why do some spend hours in the rain just to catch a glimpse of a popular actor? Why do some feel more connected to a top-selling musician than to people they see every day?

The answer to all of these questions is the same: We're naturally attracted to those who we believe are living their lives to the fullest—people who touch our souls, inspire us to take action, and are living their WHAT.

It's time to recognize that you, too, can become who you were born to be.

When you squander your time pursuing activities that provide no direct benefit, you slide further away from The Pinnacle (described in Chapter 5). As a result, you operate from a place of discontent that makes you feel even more of a need to attach yourself to those you admire.

Such distractions provide only temporary relief, though. Until you become who you were born to be, your soul will make it clear that you have yet to realize your full potential.

You can be the Star. Shake off the slumber, and awaken to the fact that all roads in the state of distraction lead to *The Slow Death of Not Being the Star*.

The Slow Death of Not Being the Star is the principle of shifting focus away from time-consuming distractions and toward the pursuit of your personal goals.

Take Inventory of Your Current Distractions

According to Nielsen, the average American watches more than 151 hours of television per month. Considering we sleep around eight hours a day, that means most of us spend more than 31 percent of our waking hours in front of a TV. But that's not the end of it. There's going to movies, attending sports events, listening to music, surfing the Internet . . . for most of us, such non-work related activities add up to over 50 percent of our waking life.

If immersing yourself in pop culture or the arts is your way of pursuing your true self, then the rest of this chapter might not apply to you. Otherwise, you may be frittering away too much of your precious time on being entertained by others. An easy way to find out is to buy a small notebook. For one week, write down how you spend the hours of each day.

Specifically, write down the time that each activity begins and ends, or simply mark the number of minutes you devote to each activity. At the end of the week, pull out your notebook and tally up how much time you devoted to pursuing your life's goals and how much you spent being distracted. The results may shock you.

Chances are you'll find that what you've been thinking of as relaxing "down-time" is actually the dominant force in your life, devouring months and years you can never get back.

The Two Ways to Use Your Time

Though we all like to think of ourselves as immortal, the truth is that our time on Earth is precious and finite. It's important to employ it wisely.

There are only two ways to use your time: *spend* it or *invest* it.

Spending *Your Time*

Spending your time is essentially the same as spending money. You have a limited amount of money, and you use it to fill various needs and desires. Once it's spent, it's no longer available for buying something else.

The same is true of your time. When you choose to devote an hour to something that doesn't advance your life's goals, you've spent that time. It's no longer yours to use, and there's nothing you can do to get it back. You weighed your options as to what you could do with your time, and you chose to spend it on an activity that didn't help you become who you need to be.

Investing *Your Time*

Investing money typically means putting your assets into stocks, real estate, and other areas that—you hope—will pay off in the long term. Similarly, investing time means focusing on activities that—you hope—will reap meaningful rewards, both as you're doing them and down the road.

In other words, investing your time means focusing on achieving your hopes and dreams.

Creation from Scratch

Instead of spending most of your time consuming the creations of others, consider focusing your time on becoming a creator. Creators are a rare breed. Only a small number of people have the patience, will, and guts necessary to take something from an idea to a tangible form and put it out there for the world to judge. Virtually everyone is a critic.

It's easy to be a critic but hard to be a creator.

Think about it. You go see a movie, watch a TV show, eat at a restaurant, and you immediately have an opinion. Your critique of this book began as soon as you started reading it. When was the last time you put something forward to be critiqued? Better yet, when was the last time you created something you weren't asked to create?

When you were a child, you created things all the time. You drew, painted, made statues out of Play-Doh, and dreamed up stories for you and your friends to take part in. If you're an artist or inventor, then you never really gave up these activities. Otherwise, you probably did. At some identifiable point, your period of creation came to a screeching halt.

It could have happened for any number of reasons. Maybe when you were five someone said your game was dumb, and from that point forward you wouldn't put yourself out on a limb again. Or maybe when you were seven your parents told you to stop getting paint on the floor, and you decided that art wasn't worth the risk of getting yelled at.

Ask yourself this question: "How long am I going to let these moments in my past control who I am today?" Your answer must be: "Not one second longer!"

Stop continuing to give power to those who have long since moved beyond whatever it was that happened years ago. The latter even includes your old self.

Don't let your past control your present and future. Whatever the reasons were that drove you to stifle your creative process—let it go.

The time for you to rekindle your creative energy is *now*. There's only one you. You're unlike anyone else on this planet, and you have unique Gifts to share and important contributions to make. If you have the talent, passion, and dedication to leverage those Gifts, you can become a creator. And maybe one day, a *Star*.

Defining What It Means to Be the *Star*

In this book, being a *Star* doesn't necessarily mean getting the lead role in a movie or selling out a rock concert. Only a select few have the talent and desire to do that.

What I mean by *Star* is connecting to your true self and living your life to the fullest. For one person, that might mean becoming an amazingly inspirational second-grade teacher. For another, it might mean being an exceptionally gentle and popular dentist.

As long as you're being true to yourself, it doesn't matter what career you star in. Nor is it important whether the stage you choose is for a relatively small audience or for millions. What counts most is that you pursue what's right for you, and you consistently give 100 percent of yourself to achieve the best performance.

If you're great at what you do, recognition will follow. And while being recognized as a *Star* might not be your goal, your example will inspire others to follow their life's path—which should be worth any temporary discomfort you experience from your celebrity.

Get a Bigger Plate

One of the most common excuses I hear for not pursuing stardom is "I don't have time. My plate is full." However, as explained earlier in this chapter, you'll typically have opportunities over the course of any day to devote a meaningful amount of time to achieving your life's goals if you want it bad enough. It's a matter of prioritizing your actions so you minimize *spending* time and focus on *investing* it.

Completing this book was a priority for me. With two young boys at home (ages six and nine), three active business units (Bold Enterprises, Bold Development, and Liquor.com), a beautiful wife, a somewhat active social life (I'm 43 . . . it ain't what it used to be), Jiu-Jitsu, golf, and other endeavors, finding time to complete this book was not always easy. As I write this paragraph, my boys are screaming in the background as one of their robot destroyer toys makes its way down the hall singing its battle cry. Though we have an office for the Bold Enterprises team, things are often quite nuts with all that's going on so I attempt to sneak in a bit of writing at home. Silence is rare.

I created this book by snatching stray hours during the day, making a habit of writing immediately after putting the kids to bed, and setting aside more than a few Saturdays and Sundays. Because completing this book was a clearly defined goal, I used every available moment I could to get it done.

Avoid the time sucks. Your life is at stake.

You'll be amazed at how much you can get done if you put your mind to it. If necessary, schedule your day so you have a clear understanding of what you'll be doing, and for how long. Take control of your time . . . and then take on more than you believe you can handle.

Get rid of the kid-size Elmo saucer that you've been balancing your life on. You're ready for a bigger plate.

Don't Feed the Trolls

A key component to becoming a Star is to *stop feeding the trolls*. While I'd love to take credit for this awesome expression, kudos goes to Randy Gage (whose *WHAT* equation is featured at the end of this chapter) for coining it. *Feeding the trolls* is Randy's analogy for what far too many creators do—listen to, respond, and be affected by those who incessantly whine and complain.

While everyone is certainly entitled to their opinion, *trolls* thrive on being included in the conversation, especially those they didn't start. Odds are good you've witnessed your share. They'll post on blogs, send emails, corner you at a networking event, and never have anything nice to say. Apparently, their goal is to ridicule creators and engage them in unproductive banter.

As you move forward on your path toward becoming a Star, you'll inevitably come across your fair share of *trolls*. When you do, take a deep breath, chuckle, disengage, and maintain your focus on adding value to our world.

How Do I Begin the Process of Being the Star?

It's easy to become enchanted with the lives of others. It's fine to be inspired by their accomplishments and to learn from their examples. But when you spend your days obsessing about those you believe are "living the dream," you lose precious time you could be investing in the creation of your own ideal life. Instead, decide to become a Star yourself, and focus your time and energy on making it happen.

Making this choice is the first vital step in your ascension to stardom. Part III of this book, "Become Who You Were Born to Be," will guide you through the next steps, which focus on identifying what you were born to do.

Life-Altering Principle #7: The Slow Death of Not Being the Star—Takeaways

- Shift your focus away from time-consuming distractions and toward the pursuit of your personal goals.
- Avoid the time sucks. Your life is at stake.
- There are only two ways to use your time—*spend* it or *invest* it.
- Stop obsessing about and living vicariously through those you believe are "living the dream." Focus your time and energy on becoming a Star yourself.
- The size of the stage is irrelevant.
- Rekindle your creative spirit and put something out there for the world to judge.
- If your plate is full, get a bigger plate—you can handle much more than you believe you can.
- Don't feed the trolls.

Realize Permanent, Positive Change—In Closing

Please accept my sincere congratulations for completing your study of *The Seven Life-Altering Principles*. Realizing permanent, positive change requires an incredible commitment. I applaud you for giving this your full attention and hope you find the rewards to be immense.

When you're ready, read Randy Gage's Case Study and move on to Part III, "Become Who You Were Born to Be." The fun is just getting started.

WHAT IS YOUR *WHAT*?
Case Study #13: Randy Gage

Randy Gage is the author of nine best-selling books, including the chart-topper *Risky Is The New Safe*. His journey from teenage drug addict, high school dropout, convict, and failed entrepreneur whose business was seized by the IRS to multimillionaire and inspirational speaker who has captivated audiences in more than 50 countries is among the most stirring rags-to-riches stories ever written.

A preeminent expert on prosperity and success, he has an uncanny ability to identify the root causes of procrastination, doubt, and uncertainty and facilitate the specific strategies required to attain one's desired results. For over 15 years, Randy has focused on research-ing, and finding powerful solutions to eliminate, the conscious and subconscious "mind viruses" that plague most individuals and organizations.

Selected as one of the 25 "Who's Hot!" speakers worldwide by *Speaker Magazine*, he is a frequent media guest who has been featured on CBS, Fox, and in dozens of magazines such as *Success, Entrepreneur,* and *Inc.* A master at unearthing hidden opportunities for creating wealth, Randy personifies his belief that your life experiences can be the stepping-stones to success if you allow them to be the learning messages they are.

Randy is a **Reinventor** and his *WHAT* is defined below. Visit RandyGage.com for more information.

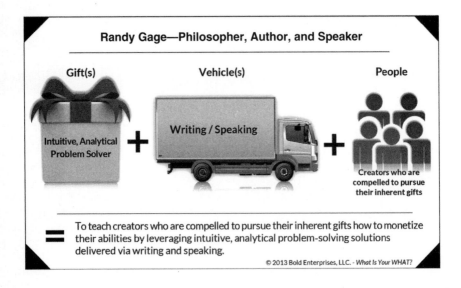

Randy Gage—Philosopher, Author, and Speaker

Gift(s)	Vehicle(s)	People
Intuitive, Analytical Problem Solver	Writing / Speaking	Creators who are compelled to pursue their inherent gifts

= To teach creators who are compelled to pursue their inherent gifts how to monetize their abilities by leveraging intuitive, analytical problem-solving solutions delivered via writing and speaking.

© 2013 Bold Enterprises, LLC. - *What Is Your WHAT?*

PART
III

Become Who You Were Born to Be

What Is Your WHAT? – An Introduction

The ideal life is in our blood and never will be still. Sad will be the day for any man when he becomes contented with the thoughts he is thinking and the deeds he is doing—where there is not forever beating at the doors of his soul some great desire to do something larger which he knows he was meant and made to do.
— Phillips Brooks

Some people call their WHAT a Gift from God. Some say they were born with their WHAT and never had any doubt about it. Others say it took them a long time to figure it out, but they finally know what their WHAT is. Still others have absolutely no idea, nor do they care, about the whole concept.

The WHAT I am referring to is the single most crucial element of your life that needs to be identified, defined, and fulfilled. Until your WHAT has been satisfied, you will roam the earth like an unsated vampire—constantly searching and forever thirsting.

Perhaps that's a bit dramatic, but your unfulfilled WHAT will absolutely affect you in a variety of unexpected ways. It could be the source of your high blood pressure, the reason why you don't feel "good enough," the cause of your general sense of loathing when you wake up, or the impetus behind your efforts at self-sabotage.

Your WHAT can't be ignored. Until you unleash your WHAT and put it front and center for the world to benefit from, it will eat away at both your body and your emotional core.

The choice is yours. You can succumb to your WHAT's greatness and its power to elevate you to the heights of your true brilliance so you can achieve your destiny, or you can lie on your deathbed knowing you squandered your most sacred Gift.

So what exactly is your WHAT?

Your WHAT is the singular combination of your innate Gifts, the Vehicle you'll leverage to share your Gifts with the world, and serving the specific audiences who'll benefit most from your Gifts. It's what comes most naturally to you, is part of your inherent blueprint, and you'd happily do without being paid a cent. When you're engaged in your WHAT, time flies by and there's nothing else you'd rather be doing.

Your WHAT reflects who you were born to be and guides you towards realizing the impact you were predestined to have on this and future generations.

Inseparable from who you are, your WHAT is your gift.

If you honor, heed, and use it wisely, it's also your gift to the world.

The WHAT Conundrum

Many on the mission of discovering and sharing their WHAT make the mistake of confusing what it is they were born to do with what it is they are currently doing. Rarely are these the same thing. Too often people forge a self-containing trench by seeking to satisfy the requirements of others, creating products and services that address the needs of their chosen market.

> *This is very different from fulfilling the requirements of what you need and then leveraging your Gift to serve others.*

This was the case for Dr. Pierre, a member of my private coaching group, The Circle of 10 (Circleof10.com). For more than 20 years, she provided consulting services to senior and C-level executives who sought concrete solutions to their operational struggles. She was well respected and very good at her trade. However, business had begun to slow, and she suddenly lacked the enthusiasm required to reignite her practice.

She joined The Circle and we began working together. As we dove deep into identifying her WHAT, she continually provided answers that reflected her current work. As I challenged her to eliminate the elevator pitch and focus on the calling of her soul, the pieces slowly began to shift. While her Gifts (Intuitive, Creative Strategist) and Vehicles (Consulting, Speaking) remained constant, the people she is most compelled to serve took a dramatic turn.

For weeks (and before we met, decades), she'd continually fought to deny who she inherently is, and sought to maintain the path she'd created to serve executives seeking corporate transformation. Eventually, however, it became clear these are not the executives she is driven to serve. Instead, her WHAT compels her to lead executives toward creating game-changing initiatives, either within or outside of their company, which provide significant benefit to society. Pursuing this focus will empower her to effect positive generational impact for millions which is exactly what she was born to do.

Discovering your WHAT is not for the meek. You have to be ready to accept it and not everyone is. Even in my workshops, many who claim to seek their WHAT maintain a Kung-Fu grip on who they've defined themselves to be.

What's deeply satisfying to me are those who wake up from a life-long slumber, discover their WHAT, and never look back.

This can be the result of an epiphany, a life-changing encounter, or a cry of frustration along the lines of Popeye's immortal, "That's all I can stands, I can't stands no more."

Andrea R., another member of The Circle, hit the wall at age 60. In her words, "I've been pretending for all of these decades I wasn't this person. Who I was reflected what everyone wanted me to be. It took me far too long to realize that I am the solution to someone else's problem."

This is profound, and bears repeating—"I am the solution to someone else's problem."

Similar to Edward Lorenz's Butterfly Effect, consider how withholding your WHAT may prevent someone from being affected by you—who then fails to affect the lives of millions of others.

Embracing the notion that your WHAT has been planted within you for not only your own good but the betterment of others is a key paradigm shift in your process of reinvention.

> *Ultimately, your WHAT isn't about you . . . it's about those you're compelled to serve.*

The simple act of freely sharing yourself is the most precious gift of all. No matter how innocuous you may feel your actions are, remember that even a small pebble dropped in the middle of a large body of water creates ripples that eventually reach the shore.

Gandhi said, "Be the change you want to see in the world." You have the power to permanently alter the world.

Start now.

The Four Types of People

There are four paths that lead toward discovering and sharing your *WHAT* with the world—and four kinds of people.

In this exercise, you will:

- Identify into which of the four groups you fit best
- Make a conscious choice about what to do with this knowledge
- Improve upon, maintain, adjust, and/or eliminate your behavior

The groups to choose from are described in the next four sections.

Birthers

Birthers are clear on what they've been born to do from a very early age. They seldom have a shadow of a doubt about what their unique Gifts are. Regardless of circumstance, their *WHAT* remains their guiding force. They may slide off course at times, but their *WHAT* always brings them back to their core.

Birthers quickly crack the code of how to make ends meet pursuing their *WHAT*. Many earn a substantial living. Birthers are completely unapologetic for the character traits they display, are often leaders, and can appear aloof because they think and behave differently from the crowd.

Fiercely independent and intolerant of excuse-driven existences, Birthers are incredibly loyal cheerleaders for those on the path to becoming who they were born to be but can be critical and irritating to those who aren't.

Relationships with Birthers involve deep, emotional ties leading to incredible closeness, or alienation that results in separate paths being pursued.

Examples of Birthers include musicians such as Paul McCartney, athletes such as LeBron James, and scientists such as Stephen Hawking.

Shifters

A Shifter seeks the missing link preventing her from creating an exceptional life. She's so close to nailing her *WHAT* equation that she can almost reach out and touch it, but there's one piece of the puzzle that's off-kilter.

Her problem might be focusing on the wrong Gift; choosing the wrong Vehicle to share her Gift; or choosing the wrong audience to serve.

The shift needed for this kind of person to find her *WHAT* is subtle—a minor tweak that will make all the difference.

Shifters can drive others batty with their obsession for a more meaningful life, but they can also be inspiring as they demand to fulfill their destinies. Shifters tend to be avid readers, continual students who seek further knowledge, bloggers, and/or media consumers.

Shifters tend to be extremely giving, happy to share their knowledge, and among the first to help others in need.

An example of a Shifter is Carol S. of Miller Beach, Indiana. Carol had been a nurse for more than 30 years when she attended The Reinvention Workshop. Though she loved her job, there was always a missing element of Carol's *WHAT* equation that nagged at her and kept her from attaining full peace and prosperity.

After a brief discussion and reviewing her equation, there was little doubt she was on target with her Gifts—*Teaching* and *Healing*; and the Vehicle she leveraged to share her Gifts with the world—*Nursing*. However, she was unclear about the specific audience who'd benefit most from her Gifts. Historically, she accepted whatever nursing opportunities were available, as opposed to knowing, and pursuing, a nursing environment that best jelled with her guiding forces. So while she'd been a respected nurse at a general hospital for more than three decades, she felt uninspired by her work.

Before long, we figured out that Carol is most compelled to serve the *disadvantaged elderly*. This was a far cry from who she was currently serving, so the disconnect was apparent.

Within months Carol landed a position at a facility that serves the disadvantaged elderly. Her life has changed dramatically for the better.

Reinventors

Reinventors are a rare breed. While few have the courage, determination, and will to become the person they were meant to be, Reinventors are ready to turn their lives completely upside down to bring their ideal life to fruition and monumentally impact the world.

A Reinventor's path is often tumultuous, though, as he seeks to move beyond his continual inner turmoil of living in denial about, or failing to pursue, who he inherently is. Before and during his transition, it's not unusual for a Reinventor to appear high-strung, emotional, out of sorts, and possibly depressed.

When his *WHAT* comes to light, however, look out. A Reinventor will then operate like a giant boulder rolling downhill, obliterating anything in his path until he's reached his goals.

It's common for Reinventors to push to the wayside anyone who tries to persuade them to hold onto the past and maintain the status quo.

An example of a Reinventor is Dr. Joe Amoia, who was described in the Introduction and whose *WHAT* appears at the end of this chapter. Joe successfully transitioned from being a full-time, well-compensated chiropractor with his own practice to becoming known as the *Smarter Dating Guy*, a dating and relationship strategist who coaches single women to find love.

Reinventors have little problem making a 180° transformation from who the world knew them to be to who they actually are.

Wanderers

I estimate over 90 percent of people are Wanderers. This isn't meant to be derogatory. It simply defines those who fit into one or more of these categories:

- Are unaware of the Gifts they've been granted
- Have been failed by society and were never taught how to tap into their unique blueprint
- Are reluctant to explore the depths of their soul due to fear, guilt, or insufficient self-esteem
- Couldn't care less about this whole concept

This does not imply that Wanderers are complacent or self-destructive.

After numerous presentations to young adults in low-income communities, audiences full of the unemployed, down-sized C-level executives, and those who can barely stand showing up at their place of employment, it's become glaringly apparent to me that most people never receive the information and encouragement needed to discover their WHAT.

This view is reinforced by the fact that when I give these audiences the choice of continuing to make ends meet by working at a job they loathe or cultivating a career they love, they unanimously choose the latter.

A possible solution is to revamp the often flawed, outdated curriculum that plagues our schools and to adequately prepare children for life. Another is to provide adults with widespread access to the necessary tools for reinvention.

Fear, on the other hand, is not as easy to fix.

Dealing with Fear

Fear—of failure, being embarrassed, losing money, not receiving the approval of others—these are just some of the reasons I repeatedly hear from those resisting their WHAT.

In contrast, my biggest fear is that when I die and meet our creator—in whatever form—I'll be told, "Son, I gave you a Gift. Because you selfishly kept your Gift within and failed to better the lives of others, you will spend eternity THERE." And THERE looks very unpleasant complete with fire and brimstone.

Alternatively, I hope to meet our creator with my heart beaming with joy and fulfillment, and be told, "Son, I gave you a Gift. Because you cherished and developed your Gift and shared your talents with as many as you could, you will spend eternity HERE." And HERE looks very pleasant complete with soft clouds and harp-playing angels.

Whatever your fears are, they are absolutely surmountable. If pursuing your WHAT is truly important to you, you'll find the solutions to overcome any self-created barriers.

Consider my acronym for *FEAR*:

Forget Everything About Reality

You can never be sure what'll happen when you embark on a new path. No matter how many scenarios you envision, the chances are things won't go as well as hoped for or as poorly as you're afraid they might. However, to deny yourself and others your inherent Gifts is a sure-fire formula for mediocrity.

Identify which group best describes you—Birthers, Shifters, Reinventors, or Wanderers—and use your knowledge to move closer to your WHAT.

Chasing Versus Creating the Opportunity

As you pursue sharing and monetizing your WHAT, try to avoid money-driven ventures that fail to stir your soul. Instead, focus on opportunities that inspire you to jump out of bed each morning while providing you with peace and prosperity.

It's common to devote years of your life to something you have no love for and *wake up* a decade later wondering what the heck happened. Pursuing money-driven ventures is an unsustainable model. Whether it's a year, five years, or two decades from now, at some point the expiration date will arrive.

Having a substantial impact on the world doesn't require you to create the next wheel. You simply have to find something you love . . . and paint it your own color.

Your WHAT Is Waiting

Identifying your WHAT usually isn't easy. But there are three simple ways you can begin facilitating this quest.

Schedule Time to Learn about Yourself

Devote focused, quiet time to identifying your WHAT. Sometimes, this is all it takes. It's a good idea to set aside a part of each day to get in touch with yourself and explore what makes you tick.

This can be done in many ways. Some people find meditation or yoga to be effective in starting inner dialogues. Others prefer a quiet walk in a park or time spent in a place of worship.

Whatever is the right approach for you, begin scheduling time to do it. If you've never tried this before, you'll soon realize that taking time out to listen to your inner self is one of the most valuable and satisfying things you can do.

Let Go of Denial

As explained in Chapter 5, you may have drifted so far from The Pinnacle that your life scarcely reflects your core identity. You may have even convinced yourself that you're a whole other person.

If the true you is buried beneath the emotional rubble of the past, it's time to dig deep and rescue it.

Explore why you've chosen to deny yourself, and everyone else, the Gift of who you really are; then do everything you can to become who you were born to be.

Vigorously Explore Your Past

When you were a toddler, you explored the world with unabashed curiosity. If you saw something that was of interest, you'd be immediately drawn to it and pursue it unreservedly, without any worry about looking silly or concern for what others thought.

Then you started being told "no." This was usually for your own good, such as the time you thought the oven was a TV.

Perhaps you loved to paint, and all of your paints were blue because that was your favorite color. Meanwhile, Mommy had a favorite color too—white, like her prized carpet.

One day, your blue paint met the white carpet—and it wasn't a Reese's Peanut Butter Cup moment when chocolate meets peanut butter and everyone's happy. Instead, you got yelled at and punished. Instinctively, you associated art with pain and buried that aspect of yourself to the nether regions never to be heard from by anyone again . . . including you.

As you grew, you learned to avoid being told "no" and getting yelled at by taking fewer chances. This resulted in only pursuing activities you were confident would garner approval. At some critical point, this may have led you to deny your true self and your natural Gifts.

If you believe this happened, think back and identify the point in your life when you took the wrong turn in the road.

Then reclaim your proper path and give yourself a second chance to live your WHAT. This chapter begins the process of understanding and discovering your WHAT. To continue your journey, proceed to Chapter 15.

What Is Your WHAT?: An Introduction—Takeaways

- Your WHAT is the innate talent that comes most naturally to you. It's your precious Gift and, if you use it wisely, it's also your Gift to the world.
- Your WHAT has chosen you. It is not that which you have chosen.
- When you're engaged in your WHAT, time flies by, and there's nothing else you'd rather be doing.
- Your WHAT reflects who you were born to be and is inseparable from who you are.
- Fulfill the requirements of what *you* need and then apply your Gifts to others.
- You are the solution to someone else's problem.
- There are four categories of people: Birthers, Shifters, Reinventors, and Wanderers. Figure out which type you are.
- Define *fear* as *Forget Everything About Reality*.
- Instead of chasing opportunities, create them.
- To begin the process of identifying your WHAT, schedule time to connect with your inner self, let go of denial, and vigorously explore your past.

WHAT IS YOUR *WHAT?*
Case Study #14: Dr. Joe Amoia

Dr. Joe Amoia is the "Smarter Dating Guy," a dating and relationship strategist who coaches single women to find love, and featured relationship expert on the hit TV series *Jerseylicious*. He began his career as a chiropractor, choosing this vocation because of his desire to help others and the findings of a *USA Today* article he read as a high school sophomore that listed the profession as a top occupation for high income and low stress.

After investing in school, opening his own practice, and serving patients for more than 15 years, Joe hit the proverbial ceiling. Concerned that his life lacked meaning and his existence would fail to have positive impact on the masses, he explored myriad personal development materials and teachers, including Wayne Dyer, Tony Robbins, and T. Harv Eker. It was at a Jack Canfield seminar, however, where his concerns were validated. Jack shared that when he was a practicing psychologist, he felt he should be doing more. This statement resonated to Joe's core.

He immediately shifted to reinvention mode, exploring various options. It wasn't until he revealed his "checklist for love" with a handful of single friends and was convinced to present his strategies that he discovered his true calling. Today, Joe offers workshops, personal coaching, and online products to serve his growing clientele.

Joe is a ***Reinventor*** and his *WHAT* is defined below. Visit SmarterDatingForWomen.com for more information.

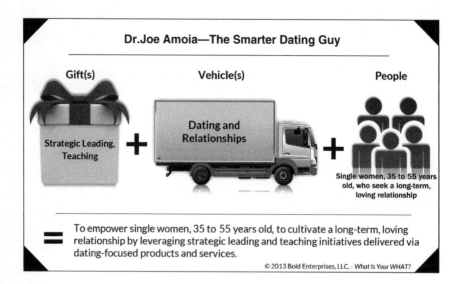

Dr.Joe Amoia—The Smarter Dating Guy

Gift(s)   Vehicle(s)   People

Strategic Leading, Teaching   +   Dating and Relationships   +   Single women, 35 to 55 years old, who seek a long-term, loving relationship

= To empower single women, 35 to 55 years old, to cultivate a long-term, loving relationship by leveraging strategic leading and teaching initiatives delivered via dating-focused products and services.

© 2013 Bold Enterprises, LLC. - *What Is Your WHAT?*

Identifying
Your *WHAT*

Step One

Take up one idea. Make that one idea your life: think of it, dream of it, live on that idea. Let the brain, muscles, nerves, every part of your body be full of that idea, and just leave every other idea alone. This is the way to success. That is the way great spiritual giants are produced.

—Swami Vivekananda

I n Chapter 14, you learned about the importance of your *WHAT* and were provided some initial suggestions for identifying it. This chapter continues the exploration in more depth, offering a multistep, proven process for revealing this vital aspect of who you are.

As explained in the Introduction, the equation for defining your *WHAT* comprises three interdependent elements.

1. Identifying your natural God-given Gifts.
2. Identifying the best Vehicle for sharing your Gifts with the world.
3. Identifying the specific audiences who'll benefit most from your Gifts.

For maximum results, each must work as a cohesive unit within an autonomous, clearly defined structure. Consider the diagram shown in Figure 15.1.

Like a tripod, each component is reliant upon the other to maintain stability and maximize the full potential of the Venn diagram. While the equation can temporarily survive without all three elements being present, eventually, performance will suffer as one or more vital pieces are removed.

For example, imagine you landed a position that involves something you're good at and you receive fair compensation to complete the assigned tasks, but it's not something you love to do. You'll always have one foot out the door as you search for a more fulfilling career.

As another example, perhaps there's something you're really good at and you love doing it, but you can't find anyone to pay you for it. This is a common situation for those in the arts, which is why you'll often hear the phrase "starving artist."

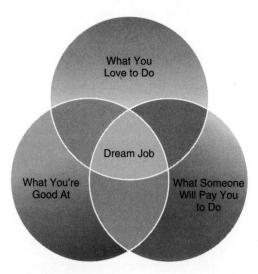

Figure 15.1   Live Within the Overlap of the Concentric Circles

Landing a dream job that allows you to live within the overlap of the concentric circles is rare. Survey the people you know and ask them if their career meets all three criteria. Few will say yes. But it's an essential goal of this book—to help you cultivate a career built around what you love to do, what you're good at, and what someone will pay you to do.

Regarding the latter, it's preferred if you're paid *a lot*. If you're constantly worried about making next month's mortgage payment or putting food on the table, it's difficult to effectively share your Gifts with the world. I believe you should be paid extraordinarily well for what you're naturally wired to do.

That said, you must be willing to serve without expectation for financial reward.

While counterintuitive, achieving success boils down to helping others get what they want out of life. Leveraging how your DNA is naturally wired to excel is the most efficient path for doing so. As Zig Ziglar said,

> *"You can have anything you want in life if you*
> *help enough people get what they want."*

Accomplishing this requires a phenomenal understanding of self—which is what we'll be tackling in this chapter.

Let's get started with Step One of the *WHAT* equation—identifying your God-given Gifts.

Step One: Things You Love to Do

Discovering your *WHAT* starts with identifying your inherent Gifts. This is achieved through a three-step process.

To begin, find a quiet place where you can think. No TV. No radio. No iPod. No kids. Just you, alone with your thoughts.

If this feels uncomfortable, that could be part of the problem. It's hard to connect with your inner self when you're continually distracted by background noise. So turn away from the distractions and focus on what's most important: the real you.

Once you're in a place of silence, think about all the things you love doing. Whatever they are, write them down in a notebook, on your laptop, or use the blank lines coming up in this section. Don't worry about anyone else reading your list; it's for you alone.

For example, it's likely you enjoy that *special time* with someone you care about. If so, write it down. Maybe you love participating in sports and playing with your kids. If so, mark those down.

Think back. What did you enjoy as a teenager? Even if you haven't done something for years, if it would still bring you pleasure, write it down.

Focus on the activities and interactions that lift your soul. Avoid listing skills you're good at simply because you've practiced them over time (e.g., washing dishes).

Dig even deeper. When you were a child, were you drawn to a certain cartoon or a certain book? What was your favorite toy? Think back to a time when you laughed hysterically—what triggered the laughter?

What's your earliest memory? Why do you think it's stuck with you when so many other memories have faded away?

As an adult, what gives you goosebumps? For me, it's witnessing someone's soul reignite. There's a specific moment in my workshop when all the elements of this process click together and you can see a person's true self reemerge. It's as if something immensely precious had been buried under years of pain, chaos, or denial. Then the key to the treasure chest is turned; when the cover is opened, you're almost blinded by the glow.

Maybe you get goosebumps when you hear a powerful singer belt out an incredible rendition of a song. Maybe it's when you pick up your child at school and his eyes light up with unbridled joy when he sees you. Perhaps it's when you come up with a really good idea and you know you've found the solution you'd been looking for. Tie these moments to descriptions that encapsulate the activity in noun or adjective form—such as *singing, listening to music, teaching, healing, entertaining.*

When recalling a special moment, try not to be too literal; look for the subtext. For example, imagine you have a fond memory of an evening spent bowling with your grandmother. Instead of writing "bowling with Grammy" on your list, broaden it to "investing time with a beloved family member."

As another example, say you closed a huge deal last year and felt really good about it. The monetary rewards are the tangibles, but what matters for this exercise is the sense of accomplishment you felt and how it enhanced your self-worth. This might be summed up as "closing a big deal."

Next, think about your character traits. Are you bold, fearless, adventurous, funny, and/or entertaining? Perhaps you're creative, intuitive, an organizer extraordinaire, and/or have a strong ear for music?

Think about how these traits are expressed through your interactions and activities. For example, if you have a strong ear for music, one of the things you probably love doing is listening to music or playing an instrument. If you're an organizer extraordinaire, maybe you love arranging people's schedules or homes.

Write down everything you love doing on the lines below:

Things I Love Doing

_____

_____

_____

_____

_____

_____

_____

_____

_____

_____

_____

_____

_____

_____

_____

_____

_____

_____

_____

_____

_____

_____

_____

_____

_____

_____

_____

_____

Look at your list. Did you miss something? Were you in denial about anything? Try to add more items to the list. This is your life—take inventory and be completely honest.

If compiling this list takes a day to complete, that's fine. If it takes a week, even better. Whenever your list includes everything you feel it should, return here to complete this exercise.

The next step is to put the activities you've identified in order of preference. My list looked like this:

1. Having *special time* with my wife.

2. Investing time with those I love.

3. Teaching others how to discover their *WHAT*.

4. Snuggling with my wife or kids.

5. Laughing, and seeing people smile and laugh.

6. Speaking to groups and businesses about how to *NICHETIZE*.

7. Inspiring others to reinvent their lives and/or companies.

8. Being bold.

9. Taking risks.

10. Listening to music and spinning records.

11. Seeing Lenny Kravitz perform.

12. Practicing Brazilian Jiu-Jitsu.

13. Thinking strategically and creatively.

14. Being outside in the warm sun.

15. Achieving my goals and having a sense of accomplishment.

16. Formulating new ideas and launching new businesses.

17. Working with entrepreneurs to help develop their businesses.

18. Attending sporting events or other live performances.

19. Mentoring.

20. Getting a really good massage.

21. Eating delicious food and enjoying a really good drink.

22. Dancing.

23. Brainstorming.

24. Writing.

25. Sleeping late.

26. Working collaboratively with others.

27. Watching sports—basketball, football, and the Ultimate Fighting Championship—and other entertainment on TV.

28. Debating.

29. Traveling and visiting new cultures.

This is what I mean about being honest. You're reading a book I wrote, and I'm listing *writing* as being way down at #24. Writing is something I love doing, but it doesn't come easily to me. That said, I couldn't be more fired up about the ideas I'm expressing, partly because they involve list items #3, #6, #7, #8, #9, #13, #17, #19 and #23.

I therefore hired Hy Bender, a phenomenal editor who's exceptional at creating great books, to go over my manuscript and make it as concise, clear, and reader-friendly as possible. (You can learn more about Hy at www.BookProposal.net.)

I want you to be just as brutally honest, because actively seeking and accepting the truth is critical if you're going to find your WHAT. You might be hesitant about admitting that you love to do something because you feel others won't approve. But if it's moral and legal, then why care what others think? Stop trying to impress people you don't really like.

Quit getting along and start making others wrong.

Go back to your list. What didn't you write down that you know needs to be there? Return to your quiet place and dig really deep.

If you've been thoroughly honest with yourself, your God-given Gifts now appear somewhere on your list. When you're ready, please order your list by preference:

Things I Love Doing, in Order of Preference

1. _____

2. _____

3. _____

4. _____

5. _____

6. _____

7. _____

8. _____

9. _____

10. _____

11. _____

12. _____

13. _____

14. _____

15. _____
16. _____
17. _____
18. _____
19. _____
20. _____
21. _____
22. _____
23. _____
24. _____
25. _____
26. _____
27. _____
28. _____
29. _____
30. _____

Step Two: Things You Hate to Do

The next step in the process of identifying your inherent Gifts requires you to be totally honest about all the things you *hate* to do. If you're clear about what activities you despise, you can establish a strong foundation for moving your life forward by starting to let them go.

For example, maybe you abhor filing. You consider it mindless, time-consuming, unfulfilling work; and you always end up with a paper cut. Standing in front of a file cabinet with a 12-inch stack of pages to put away using some arcane system makes you want to light a match and set them on fire.

Whatever it is that pushes your buttons, write them down in a notebook, on your laptop, or use the blank lines coming up in this section.

Also, reflect on *why* you deplore an activity. Did you see or experience something that traumatized you as a child or that you were teased about as a teenager? Did you do something when you were younger that so upset you—for example, working at your family's slaughterhouse—that you swore to never do it again? And are you doing something similar now regardless?

What regular occurrences in your life make your blood curdle? Do you tell your boss how great he is, even though you'd like to kick him down a flight of stairs?

Are you "friends" with the couple two houses down who you can't stand simply because you don't want to have an unharmonious relationship with neighbors?

Whatever it is that eats at you, write it down. Even if you worry others might see it as petty, include it. This exercise takes place without judgment. The key is to acknowledge your thoughts and feelings.

Again, tie these moments to descriptions that encapsulate the activity in noun or adjective form—for example, *cleaning, watching TV, eating unhealthy food, being around miserable people, shopping.* When you're ready, please create your list:

Things I Hate Doing

You may be amazed at how freeing it is to get all this down on paper. Activities you perform regularly that you've never admitted deeply bother you will jump out and shout at you.

Get it all out. Don't hold anything back. As with Step One, take as much time as you need, whether it's a day or a week. What matters is writing it all down.

The next step is to put the activities you've identified in order, from most to least distasteful. My list looked like this:

1. Dealing with minutiae.
2. Being affected by others' lack of integrity (e.g., people not honoring their commitments).
3. Being with people who minimize or mitigate my feelings.
4. Witnessing racism, discrimination, and other forms of oppression.
5. Being lied to.
6. Affecting someone in a negative manner.
7. Hearing people complain, even if they're justified.
8. Being yelled at or treated in a disrespectful manner.
9. Being treated poorly or unfairly.
10. Disappointing others by not delivering on my promises or projections.
11. Sitting at a desk for a prolonged period of time.
12. Having to clean up, or cover for, other people's problems.
13. Dealing with governmental or corporate bureaucracy.
14. Being late or having to wait for others.
15. Paying bills or doing accounting.
16. Being awakened out of a solid slumber or having to wake up early.
17. Engaging in any sort of office work.
18. Placating people for whom I have no respect.
19. Tolerating really bad music.
20. Wasting money on crappy food.
21. Killing insects.
22. Dealing with my inability to breathe through my nose.
23. Dealing with my lower back pain.
24. Dealing with my tinnitus.
25. Cleaning toilets.

When you're ready, please order your list from most to least distasteful:

Things I Hate Doing, in Order of Distaste

1. _____
2. _____
3. _____
4. _____
5. _____
6. _____
7. _____
8. _____
9. _____
10. _____
11. _____
12. _____
13. _____
14. _____
15. _____
16. _____
17. _____
18. _____
19. _____
20. _____
21. _____
22. _____
23. _____
24. _____
25. _____
26. _____
27. _____
28. _____
29. _____
30. _____

Now that you've got your annoyances down on paper, take a closer look. Do all of the items ring true? Did you miss anything? Were you being completely honest?

U.S. Senate Chaplain Peter Marshall opened a prayer session in 1947 by noting, "Unless we stand for something, we shall fall for anything." What you wrote down are the things you shouldn't tolerate, but you probably "fall" for most of them.

Think about how you spend a typical day, and figure out how much time is devoted to these activities you despise.

Now understand that you have to stop doing most of these things—because life is too short, and they're slowly killing you.

> *Every minute you engage in an activity you abhor reduces*
> *your life expectancy by an equal amount of time.*

You're probably getting paid for doing a lot of these things. Comedian Drew Carey once said, "I belong to a therapy group for people who hate their jobs. It's called *everybody*. And it meets in a bar." But whatever money you're making probably isn't worth the cost to your happiness, health, and sense of identity.

Of course, letting go of these drags on your life can take time, especially if the apparent alternatives are even worse.

Short term, try to establish a frame of mind that lets you do these things with minimal discomfort.

Long term, however, you should strive for creative solutions that let you drop these activities for good.

Another thing to consider is how you've put up with these self-destructive activities for so long. Your inner self must have been crying out to you to stop, and you responded by slapping a muzzle on it. When you tell your deepest self to shut up and find ways to rationalize your behavior, you risk committing great harm not only to yourself, but to others.

After all, isn't this how evil in the world takes place? People shut themselves off to what they know in their souls is right and make up excuses to perform acts that horrify them on some level. The more they do it, the bigger the excuses they create so they can live with the lies. This is why it's imperative to listen to your gut.

> **When something shakes you to your core and your inner voice screams at you**
> **to stop, pay attention. This is your soul sending a direct message.**

You might think of your rationalizing brain as your Devil (I call this the Voice of Conjecture) and your soul as your Angel. Whether or not you listen to your soul will determine the quality of your existence.

The list you just created came from your inner Angel. Heed it.

Step Three: The Seven Seeds of Your Soul

This section is where your previous work pays off in helping to identify your inherent Gifts. Please grab your notebook, laptop, or dog-ear the pages that contain your final lists of *Things I Love Doing* and *Things I Hate Doing*, as you'll be referring to them frequently during this exercise.

Let's start with the top item on your list of *Things I Love Doing*. Read it to yourself a couple of times so you can really feel the words.

Next, ask yourself each of the six questions below as it relates to the activity. Each answer should be a definitive *yes* or *no*. Trust yourself and don't second-guess. Your first answer will almost always be right:

1. Even if you didn't get paid a cent for it, would you still do this?
2. Would doing this inspire you every day?
3. Does doing this come as naturally to you as breathing?
4. Do you feel you've been given a special Gift to do this?
5. Does time seem to fly by when you're engaged in this activity?
6. Can you possibly make money doing this?

People often have difficulty answering *yes* or *no* to Questions #4 and #6. For Question #4, keep in mind that while you might not yet be a master of this activity, if you feel passionately about it and/or spend a lot of time engaging in it, you may have been given a special Gift to do it. In such cases your answer to Question #4 is likely to be *yes*, but you must be brutally honest.

For example, perhaps you identified *traveling* as one of the things you love doing. Although everyone has the ability to travel, only a small percentage enjoys spending most of their time on the road or in the air. If getting paid to see the world lights your fire, then your answer for this activity is *yes*; otherwise, it's *no*.

For Question #6, answer whether you can *possibly* make money performing the activity, not whether you're currently doing so. If you have a genuine Gift, you can monetize virtually any hobby, interest, or endeavor and, therefore, your answer would be *yes*. If you disagree with this statement, please email me at Steve@SteveOlsher.com and I'll teach you how to make money doing what you love to do.

If *any* of your answers to these first six questions is *no*, cross out the activity and move to the next item on your list of *Things I Love Doing*. Again, read the activity to yourself a couple of times and then run it through the six questions.

Continue this process until you reach an activity that results in a *yes* to all six questions. When you arrive at such an item, circle it, and then ask yourself this final question:

> ### *Does performing this activity involve anything on my list of Things I Hate Doing?*

To help make this clearer, let me walk you through what my process looked like. As you may recall, the top item on my list of *Things I Love Doing* was

> ### *Having special time with my wife.*

My answers to the first six questions were as follows:

1. Even if you didn't get paid a cent for it, would you still do this? **YES**
2. Would doing this inspire you every day? **YES**
3. Does doing this come as naturally to you as breathing? **YES**
4. Do you feel you've been given a special Gift to do this? **NO**
5. Does time seem to fly by when you're engaged in this activity? **YES**
6. Can you possibly make money doing this? **NO**

It would be nice to think that I've been given a special Gift and could make money at it, but total honesty is required. Therefore, I had to go to the next item on my *Things I Love Doing* list, which is

> ### *Investing time with those I love.*

Again, I couldn't answer *yes* to all six questions, so I proceeded to the next item on my list:

> ### *Teaching others how to discover their WHAT.*

For this activity, my answers to the first six questions were as follows:

1. Even if you didn't get paid a cent for it, would you still do this? **YES**
2. Would doing this inspire you every day? **YES**
3. Does doing this come as naturally to you as breathing? **YES**
4. Do you feel you've been given a special Gift to do this? **YES**
5. Does time seem to fly by when you're engaged in this activity? **YES**
6. Can you possibly make money doing this? **YES**

A clean sweep! All of those *yes* answers meant I could circle it and go on to the final question:

7. Does performing this activity involve anything on your list of *Things I Hate Doing*?

For each item on my *Hate* list, I read my beloved activity out loud first (as shown by the first two examples below) and then matched it against the despised activity. Here were my answers:

1. Does teaching others how to discover their WHAT require me to "Deal with minutiae?" **NO**
2. Does teaching others how to discover their WHAT involve my "Being affected by others' lack of integrity (e.g., people not honoring their commitments)?" **NO**
3. Surrounding myself with those who minimize or mitigate my feelings. **NO**
4. Witnessing racism, discrimination, and other forms of oppression. **NO**
5. Being lied to. **NO**
6. Affecting someone in a negative manner. **NO**
7. Hearing people complain, even if they're justified. **YES**
8. Being yelled at or treated in a disrespectful manner. **NO**
9. Being treated poorly or unfairly. **NO**
10. Disappointing others by not delivering on my promises or projections. **NO**
11. Sitting at a desk for a prolonged period of time. **NO**
12. Having to clean up, or cover for, other people's problems. **NO**
13. Dealing with governmental or corporate bureaucracy. **NO**
14. Being late or having to wait for others. **NO**
15. Paying bills or doing accounting. **NO**
16. Being awakened out of a solid slumber or having to wake up early. **NO**
17. Engaging in any sort of office work. **YES**
18. Placating people for whom I have no respect. **NO**
19. Tolerating really bad music. **NO**
20. Wasting money on crappy food. **NO**
21. Killing insects. **NO**
22. Dealing with my inability to breathe through my nose. **NO**

23. Dealing with my lower back pain. **NO**

24. Dealing with my tinnitus. **NO**

25. Cleaning toilets. **NO**

For the beloved activity to pass the criteria of The Seven Seeds of Your Soul, it has to match *no more than two* of your hated activities. If you answer *yes* three or more times, cross off the activity, and continue the process with the next item on your *Things I Love Doing* list.

If you answer *yes* less than three times, however, double circle the activity because you'll be returning to it. Meanwhile, continue the process by moving to the next item on your *Things I Love Doing* list.

You may wonder why I'm not insisting on a clean sweep of *no*'s for the *Things I Hate Doing* list. The fact is virtually any activity you engage in will include aspects you dislike. That's just reality. But the discomfort level has to be low enough to be tolerable. By my being able to answer *yes* to the first six questions, and by answering *yes* no more than twice to the seventh question, I concluded that activity #3 on my list—*Teaching others how to identify their WHAT*—satisfied the criteria of The Seven Seeds.

I then went on to review the 26 remaining items on my *Things I Love Doing* list to see if any other activity met the criteria. Only two others did: #6, *Speaking to groups and businesses about how to NICHETIZE* and #7, *Inspiring others to reinvent their lives and/or companies.*

This exercise may be time-consuming if you've created an extremely long list (in which case, kudos for enjoying so many things), but it's well worth the investment. It's possible that your inherent Gifts won't appear in the first half or even the first two-thirds of your list, so be patient and work through every item.

Bottom line: These are the first steps of the most important process in this entire book. Don't rush it. And no matter how long it takes, see it through to completion. Your life is at stake, and the rewards are incalculable.

Time to get to it!

Follow the steps described, and write the activities that you double circled here:

1. _____

2. _____

3. _____

If after going through the entire process you've been unable to identify *any* activity that satisfies The Seven Seeds of Your Soul, please return to the beginning of this chapter and start again . . . in a very quiet place, taking all the time you need. Your Gifts are there for you to discover. Commit to this exercise and you'll find them.

Conversely, if you came up with more than three results, the chances are you weren't sufficiently honest during the process—for example, you may have created too short a list of things you hate to do. In this case, please return to the start of this chapter and try again.

Eliminating items from your list is not always easy. *Being bold* and *taking risks* are two items that personify who I am (my DJ name was Mr. Bold), and it pained me that they didn't qualify. But the reality is I haven't been given a special Gift to be bold or take risks. Anyone can engage in these activities; and many do.

Once you've identified three or fewer activities, the last step is to choose the specific nouns or adjectives that best define your Gifts. These will typically be the first words of your activity statements. In reviewing my discoveries—*Teaching others how to identify their WHAT, Speaking to groups and businesses about how to NICHETIZE,* and *Inspiring others to reinvent their lives and/or companies*—the first words were *Teaching, Speaking,* and *Inspiring.*

At first I considered whether every one of these words was a separate Gift, as each resonated to my core. After thinking more deeply, though, I realized they're all part of an over-arching theme: *Communication.* And *Communication* is my true Gift.

That said, the three words remained individually important because they indicated what Vehicles I'd use to share my Gifts with the world. (Much more about Vehicles appears in the next chapter.)

Review your results, and write your Gifts below using one or, at most, two words for each. Also, if possible, identify an over-arching theme:

1. _____

2. _____

3. _____

Many of my clients find identifying their Gifts provides one of the most powerful and satisfying feelings of their lives.

If you can pinpoint your Gifts and complete your WHAT equation, you'll probably feel like you've thrown a 500-pound bag of sand off your shoulders. It's often a very emotional experience.

Tania M., another Circle of 10 member, described finding her Gifts this way: "I cried when I saw the words in front of me. Tapping into my Gifts was extremely emotional, fulfilling, and scary all at once. Being so close to my core, and understanding how I'm wired, is more powerful than I can express."

Similarly, seeing your own Gifts on paper should move you and put a fire in your belly.

If this isn't the case, the chances are you haven't identified your Gifts yet. Return to the start of this chapter, and keep at it until you feel down to your bones that you've found your true Gifts.

To recap, here are the steps required to identify your Gifts:

1. Create a list of things you love to do.

2. Create a list of things you hate to do.

3. Run the list of things you love to do against the first six questions from The Seven Seeds of Your Soul. Circle the items that qualify and scratch off those that don't.

4. Once you've identified the items to which you answered *yes* for the first six questions, run them against Question #7 and your *Things I Hate Doing* list. Double circle the items that qualify and scratch off those that don't.

5. Write down the activities that satisfy the criteria for The Seven Seeds (there should be three or less).

6. Pinpoint the nouns or adjectives, and the overarching theme, that defines your Gift(s).

I understand this process may be confusing. If you reread this chapter and remain unclear about what to do, please visit WhatIsYourWhat.com/resources to watch the video titled "Step One for Discovering Your *WHAT*." This short tutorial takes you step-by-step through exactly what to do.

When you've successfully completed this chapter, please proceed to Chapter 16 to embark on Steps 2 and 3.

Identifying Your WHAT: Step 1—Takeaways

- Shift from merely being awake to being *alive*.
- Find your sweet spot of life where the concentric circles overlap.
- Stop trying to impress people you don't really like.
- If you stand for nothing, you'll fall for anything.
- Every minute you engage in an activity you abhor reduces your life expectancy by an equal amount of time.
- The quality of your existence is determined largely by whether or not you listen to your gut.
- Use The Seven Seeds of Your Soul to discover your God-given Gifts.
- Pinpoint the nouns or adjectives and the over-arching theme that defines your Gift(s).

WHAT IS YOUR *WHAT?*
Case Study #15: Jack Canfield

Jack Canfield is the founder and chairman of The Canfield Training Group, a world-renown organization that teaches entrepreneurs, educators, corporate leaders, and motivated individuals how to accelerate the achievement of their personal and professional goals. He is also the founder of The Foundation for Self-Esteem, which provides self-esteem resources and trainings to social workers, welfare recipients, and human resource professionals; founder and former CEO of Chicken Soup for the Soul Enterprises, a billion-dollar empire that encompasses licensing, merchandising, and publishing activities around the globe; and, founder of the Transformational Leadership Council.

He began his career as a teacher at an inner city Chicago high school. Perplexed by his students' general lack of motivation to learn, he sought solutions that would motivate them to fully engage. This pursuit led him to W. Clement Stone and a two-year stint working at his foundation. There, he was exposed to powerful personal development strategies including, visualization, goal setting, the Law of Attraction, and establishing clearly defined values—invaluable tools he would subsequently share with his students.

Over the ensuing years, Jack taught for Insight and eventually created his own Growth Center and developed Self-Esteem Seminars to serve others in a large, group-training environment. In 1993, he wrote *Chicken Soup for the Soul* and, in 2006, *The Success Principles*. With over 500 million copies in print, they are among the most commercially successful books ever released. His life-purpose statement—*"To inspire and empower people to live their highest vision in the context of love and joy in harmony with the highest good of all concerned"*—reflects not only his guiding belief, but also the daily mantra he embodies to transform the lives of millions.

Jack is a **Reinventor** and his *WHAT* is defined below. Visit www.JackCanfield.com for more information.

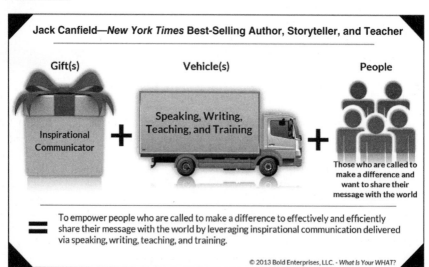

Jack Canfield—*New York Times* Best-Selling Author, Storyteller, and Teacher

Gift(s)	Vehicle(s)	People
Inspirational Communicator	Speaking, Writing, Teaching, and Training	Those who are called to make a difference and want to share their message with the world

To empower people who are called to make a difference to effectively and efficiently share their message with the world by leveraging inspirational communication delivered via speaking, writing, teaching, and training.

© 2013 Bold Enterprises, LLC. - *What Is Your WHAT?*

Identifying Your WHAT

Steps Two and Three

I thought I'd never accomplish anything really wonderful, that I'd have an ordinary life and it scared me.

—David Geffen

Now that you've completed Step One of the three-step process for identifying your WHAT, you should have a solid grasp of your inherent Gifts. Step Two requires you to identify your *Vehicle*. While your Gifts represent your innate skills and abilities, the Vehicle is the physical action or platform you'll use to share your Gifts with the world.

Examples of Vehicles include

- Speaking
- Teaching (e.g., yoga, martial arts, traditional education, coaching)
- Nursing
- Healing (e.g., Reiki, massage therapy, counseling)
- Writing
- Protecting (e.g., police officer, fire fighter)

- Creating (e.g., painting, sculpting, writing)
- Athletics
- Performing Arts (e.g., music, acting, dancing)
- Entrepreneurial endeavors
- Assembling (e.g., politics, creating a nonprofit, community organizing)

The key to identifying your Vehicle is to consider how, and when, you're most at peace.

For instance, some people love the stage. No matter where they are or who the audience is, they want to be front and center. For this group, speaking or teaching may be a perfect Vehicle, as when they're engaged in this activity they feel the most alive.

Others, however, loathe public speaking; the idea of all eyes being on them makes their skin crawl. This group might prefer communicating through blogs or books, or simply one-on-one.

Take a few minutes to consider when you achieve true inner peace and how you want to share your Gifts.

Identify Your *Vehicle* — Step Two

For now, choose just *one* Vehicle. Once you've established expertise, notoriety, and financial success by exhausting the reach of your selected Vehicle, you can expand on the ways you serve your audience. Keep in mind that many renowned experts, such as Rick Warren and Paolo Coelho, began in this exact manner: serving a particular group in one specific way first and then pursuing other Vehicles to spread their message. At a later date you may find that, as your Gifts and platform evolve, you choose an entirely different Vehicle.

Michael Strahan is a perfect example. An all-pro defensive lineman with the New York Giants, Strahan leveraged his innate physical and psychological Gifts to become one of the greatest to ever play the game. After retiring from football, though, Strahan reinvented his life by tapping into other natural talents, focusing on *Entertaining* as his core Gift and *Media* as the Vehicle he leverages to share his Gift with the world.

Strahan went on to become a spokesman for Subway restaurants, cohost of top-rated TV show *FOX NFL Sunday*, and cohost of *LIVE! with Kelly & Michael*. He probably never dreamed 20 years ago that this is where his Gifts would lead him.

As to whether Strahan's true WHAT was his Gift of *Athletics* and his Vehicle of *Football* vs. his Gift of *Entertaining* and his Vehicle of *Media* is an interesting question. Maybe his over-arching Gift is *Performing*, and he simply found different ways of expressing that. There's no doubt that the years he spent in front of football fans and the press were great training for his media career.

Too many people get hung up on having to choose just *one* Gift and *one* Vehicle, and ultimately never choose *anything*. "There's so much more to me than that!" is a statement I often hear. It's certainly true that there are many ways you're able to share your Gift with the world, but you must start somewhere before expanding to other endeavors and Vehicles.

In our instant gratification society, it's common to want to be immediately seen as being at the pinnacle of one's profession. But this is unlikely to happen.

What *will* happen if you're willing to work at honing both your Gifts and your chosen Vehicle is that you'll begin to manifest meaningful results. Growth is a natural byproduct of forward motion.

Conversely, organisms that don't move will eventually die. Human beings are no different.

Don't quit before you take your first step. Victory lies in claiming your position on the road, not waiting for the finish line to appear and crossing it.

That's in part because, as explained in Chapter 9, the finish line is usually an illusion. No matter when you believe you've "arrived," the line will continue to elude you as you intentionally, or unintentionally, move it further down your path. It's simply how we're wired—we're always striving for more. That's why "The Destination *Is* the Road and The *Journey* Is the Destination."

So get out of *park*, put yourself in *drive*, hit the gas . . . and start your journey.

The equation you create today might not come close to reflecting the equation you have in place five years from now. However, the equation you put in place today will absolutely empower you to move forward to where you belong.

Please choose the *one* Vehicle you'll leverage for the immediate future. Again, if you'd like examples, flip to the end of each chapter of this book where you'll find a Case Study of someone brilliantly living his or her *WHAT*.

Whenever you're ready, please write your answer below:

The Vehicle I will (initially) use to share my Gifts with the world is this:

_____

If you're certain that multiple Vehicles are appropriate for you, look for synergies among them so you can either combine them into a single Vehicle or pursue them all in ways that enhance each other.

For instance, if your Vehicles are *Cooking* and *Teaching*, you can pursue becoming a master chef and, once you know enough, pass along what you've learned and teach aspiring chefs. You'll probably find you learn as much from your students as they do from you, so your teaching will ultimately make you an even better chef.

As another example, if your two Vehicles are *Baseball* and *Writing*, you could be a sports writer who focuses on baseball, or a baseball player who writes a blog to increase fan interest in his career.

One of my participants in The Reinvention Workshop identified *Cooking, Photography*, and *Travel* as her Vehicles. Among the ideas we brainstormed was her becoming a traveling photographer who captures images of people enjoying the foods they love. She was completely inspired by the idea and began organizing her life to achieve this goal.

If the synergy between your Vehicles isn't evident, or if you're unmoved by what you've identified, you'll have to be more creative. You might even pursue different Vehicles on parallel tracks for a while to learn which draws you in the most. Mark Twain wrote, "The difference between the right word and the almost right word is the difference between lightning and the lightning bug." To make a meaningful difference, you'll eventually need to pinpoint what stirs your soul.

What Is Your WHAT?—Step Three

The third part of the equation requires you to become clear on who you're most compelled to serve. Many have brought their *WHAT* into focus by identifying the specific audience who'll benefit from their Gifts.

A simple way to start this process is by reflecting on who you are and what you've experienced. This can help reveal the groups for whom you feel a natural connection.

To start, read the identifiers that follow and ask yourself what words or phrases describe you for each. For example, for the first item *family role*, identify your roles in your family: for example, *parent, spouse, daughter, brother*. Write your answer directly below the identifier, then move to the next item.

Most answers will be obvious. Some will require introspection.

When you've worked through all the items, think about other ways in which you can self-identify, and then write down the applicable attributes, beliefs, and passions in the last space shown.

Please begin:

- Family role (e.g., mother, father, sister, brother, aunt, uncle, grandparent)

  _____

- Survivor (e.g., illness, abuse, trauma, death of a loved one, injury, financial peril)

  _____

- Award winner (e.g., sports, business, education)

  _____

- Personal reinvention (e.g., career change, personal life overhaul)

  _____

- Physical attributes (e.g., tall, short, fat, skinny)

  _____

- Health ailments (e.g., disease, sex-related issues)

  _____

- Cultural background (e.g., African, Caucasian, Asian, American Indian)

  _____

- Social and economic inequities (e.g., poverty, education, healthy food options)

  _____

- Religion (e.g., Catholic, Jewish, Buddhist)

  _____

- Hobbies (e.g., sculpting, sewing, Sudoku, music, martial arts, reading)

  _____

- Volunteering (e.g., PTA, networking groups, Red Cross, Habitat For Humanity)

  _____

- Political views (e.g., Democratic, Republican, pro- or anti-abortion, pro- or anti-gun)

  _____

Other important facets of who I am, what I believe in, and what's most important to me:

_____

_____

_____

_____

_____

_____

_____

_____

_____

Next, create a statement that summarizes your findings. The following are three examples of *Who I Am* statements.

Who I Am *Example #1*

I am a father, son, and uncle who lost my parents when I was very young.

A successful athlete in high school and college, I excelled in baseball and football, and was a key player on our Division III championship football team.

Two years ago, I lost the job I held for two decades and had to completely start over in a new career.

Today I'm an assistant football coach at a local high school.

During this transition, I became a practicing Buddhist, lost 20 pounds, and instituted a vegan diet.

I love to paint, volunteer at homeless shelters, and believe that everyone should have an equal opportunity to contribute to society.

Who I Am *Example #2*

I am a mother and daughter who spent the first 10 years of my life being transferred from foster home to foster home.

I never knew my parents but, instinctively, I am a survivor. This mentality helped me greatly when I left a physically abusive husband after 10 years of marriage, packing my belongings and two young children in the car and driving away in the middle of the night.

After divorcing and settling in a small Kansas town, I found work as a secretary at a manufacturing company, and have slowly worked my way through the ranks. My children both graduated from Ivy League schools, and I am a very well compensated executive.

While I believe in Christ, I believe in self first, and want to empower other women to tap their strength, leave abusive relationships, and help them on their journey.

Who I Am *Example #3*

I am a daughter and sister.

I'm in graduate school studying to be an economist. I love numbers and people, as well as the challenge of finding answers where practical solutions are non-existent.

Raised Jewish, I haven't been to synagogue since I was 14.

In my spare time I practice yoga and travel to study under many of the world's foremost yogis. I recently started an evening yoga class for graduate students and find it very fulfilling.

I also volunteer at the local Y, teaching basic fitness to seniors.

Recently, a drunk driver killed a friend, and I'm furious that more isn't done to prevent people from driving while intoxicated.

Your Own Who I Am *Statement*

Write your own statement in the space that follows. Refer back to your list of attributes, beliefs, and passions to do so.

_____

_____

_____

_____

_____

_____

_____

_____

_____

_____

Choosing Your Audience

Now think about whether a combination of your findings identifies a specific audience who'll benefit most from your Gifts. Here are a few examples to consider:

- You were born into poverty but were driven to break the generational grip of economic struggle. After excelling in high school, you financed college with grants, scholarships, and full-time jobs, eventually earning a Bachelor's degree. The idea of serving those with limited means by teaching them the required steps to earn their college degree puts fire in your soul.
- You're a 50-year-old woman with diabetes who lost 100 pounds over the past 12 months and want to share your strategies with others.
- You're an expert male gymnast who has won local and national competitions, and would like to share your knowledge with aspiring 12- to 14-year-old Level 10 Olympic hopefuls.

The more specific you can be, the easier it'll be to share your knowledge, cultivate a legion of followers, get paid exceptionally well for your expertise, and achieve peace and prosperity.

You may often find yourself drawn to serving more than one group. In "*Who I Am* Example #3," the woman studying to be an economist clearly has a passion for yoga, is fired up to prevent intoxicated drivers from getting behind the wheel, and is in graduate school pursuing an advanced degree in Economics. It may be difficult for her to select just one group to focus on.

In such cases, I recommend turning to Kurt Lewin's *Approach-Approach Theory of Conflict*. This is a process for choosing between two or more equally attractive goals.

In Example #3, the woman must choose between focusing on economics, yoga, or eliminating drunk driving. Here's the process she might go through:

> Economics vs. yoga: If I can only choose one, which do I select? I love yoga more, so I choose that. She then moves on to the next decision: Yoga vs. eliminating drunk driving: If I can only choose one, which do I select? I still love yoga more, so I choose that.

This simple yet highly effective process can help you identify which pursuit you'll initially undertake.

Again, you can always revisit your options in the future. For now, however, begin with one choice and pursue it with vigor until your fire has run its course, or you recognize that the choice made is incongruent with who you are.

Referring back to your statement and, if necessary, enacting the *Approach-Approach Theory of Conflict*, identify the subset of the population you have an affinity for and feel compelled to help, teach, empower, and/or serve. Describe your audience in the space that follows:

_____

_____

_____

Congratulations! If you've done all the recommended work, you have now completed the three steps required to discover your *WHAT*:

1. Identifying your natural God-given Gifts.

2. Identifying the best Vehicle for sharing your Gifts with the world.

3. Identifying the specific audience who'll benefit most from your Gifts.

Please write your findings on Figure 16.1. Enter your name above the top line. If you have a moniker to go with your *WHAT* (e.g., America's Reinvention Expert), include it as well. Reference the examples at the end of each chapter if necessary.

If you don't feel comfortable with your answers or haven't yet completed all the steps, revisit each section where you had difficulty. Stick with this process until you're ready to move forward.

Once everything is solidly in place, please continue to the final step—formulating your concise statement that encapsulates the three elements you've identified.

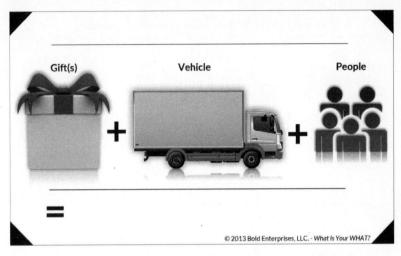

Figure 16.1 Use This Template to Enter Your Findings

What Is Your WHAT?—The Final Step

While each element of your *WHAT* can stand alone as a guiding component of who you inherently are, a well-defined, cohesive statement is substantially more powerful than the sum of its parts. Creating a one-sentence summation that ties together your findings will provide an easy-to-reference mantra that keeps you focused on the core objective you've identified as your reason for being.

This statement defines the following:

- How you'll impact those you're compelled to serve
- Who they are
- Your God-given gifts
- The Vehicle you'll leverage to reach them

An example of a completed statement comes from Suzanne Evans, a renowned speaker, business coach, and creator of next-level live events such as *Be The Change*. Suzanne's Case Study appears at the end of this chapter. Suzanne's *WHAT* and summation statement are shown in Figure 16.2

Let's take a closer look at Suzanne's statement in relation to each of the elements, beginning with "How will you impact those you're compelled to serve?"

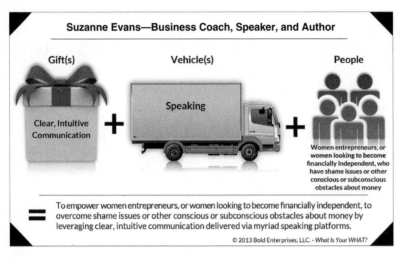

Figure 16.2 Suzanne Evans—Business Coach, Speaker, and Author

The first word of your summation statement will always be "To" followed by a verb (call to action). Typical action words for a summation statement include these:

- Empower
- Teach
- Prepare
- Engage
- Entertain
- Foster
- Encourage
- Inspire
- Alter
- Motivate
- Create
- Train
- Provide
- Lead

Reflecting on your Gifts, Vehicle, and Audience, think about what you hope to accomplish. Do you want to *teach* those you're most compelled to serve to achieve something specific? Do you want to *entertain* them? Do you want to *motivate* them to complete a certain action? Suzanne identified *empower*.

Consider your desired outcome and fill in the blank with the pertinent action:

"To _____ (*action*)."

Next, identify who you're most compelled to serve. This answer appears in Step Three of the three-step process for identifying your WHAT. In Suzanne's statement, she identified "women entrepreneurs, or women looking to become financially independent." Please be specific, including as much demographic detail as possible: age, affliction, economic status, key concern, and so on. Fill in the blanks below with both of your answers:

"To _____ (*action*) _____
_____(*who*)."

Now identify what you'll help them achieve. What happens after they work with you or are exposed to your teachings? In other words, what's the result you want to help them accomplish? The result Suzanne seeks is "To empower women entrepreneurs, or women looking to become financially independent, to overcome shame issues or other conscious or subconscious obstacles about money."

Fill in the blanks below with all three of your answers:

"To _____ (*action*) _____
_____(*who*)
to _____ (*result*)."

The second to last step is to describe your expertise and how you'll help your audience attain the desired result. Refer to Step One and the Gifts you identified to do this.

It's often easiest to begin this section with "by leveraging." For example, Suzanne's statement includes "by leveraging clear, intuitive communication." Fill in the blanks below with all four of your answers:

"To _____ (*action*) _____
_____(*who*)
to _____ (*result*)
by leveraging _____(*your innate Gifts*)."

The last step is to specify how you'll deliver your expertise. In other words, what Vehicle will you use to share your Gifts? Please refer to your answers from Step Two to identify how the world will receive your message.

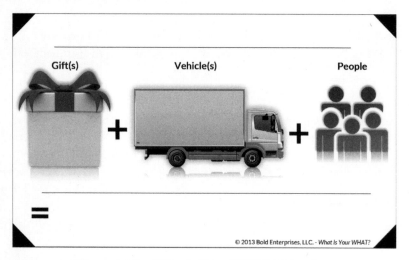

Figure 16.3   What Is Your WHAT? Template

Suzanne will help those she's compelled to serve by delivering her Gifts "via myriad speaking platforms." Please complete your summation statement by filling in all of the blanks below.

"To _____(action) _____
_____(who)
to _____ (result)
by leveraging _____(your innate Gifts)
delivered via _____ (method of delivery)."

With your summation statement now complete, please use the template in Figure 16.3 to enter your findings and answer life's most important question: **What Is Your WHAT?**

If you're still having trouble identifying your WHAT, or understanding how to move forward with the discoveries you've made, enlist those in your closest circle. Often what's hardest for you to see is obvious to others.

Commit to this process and eventually your WHAT will become clear. When it does, life as you know it will never be the same.

Identifying Your WHAT:
Steps Two and Three—Takeaways

- Identify the Vehicle you'll leverage to share your Gifts with the world.
- For now, focus on pursuing just one Vehicle. If necessary, look for synergies among multiple Vehicles.
- Don't quit before even getting started.
- Figure out who your audience is by identifying your attributes, beliefs, and passions.
- If necessary, use Kurt Lewin's *Approach-Approach Theory of Conflict* to make your final choice.
- Create a well-defined, cohesive statement that encapsulates your WHAT.
- Answer life's most important question: **What Is Your WHAT?**

WHAT IS YOUR *WHAT?*
Case Study #16: Suzanne Evans

Suzanne Evans is a leading business coach, strategist, speaker, and founder of the Global Impact Project—a non-profit serving women worldwide in education, entrepreneurship, and equality. In less than four years, her company has grown to serve over 30,000 clients enrolled in her wealth and business-building programs and to #225 on the Inc. 500 list.

Beginning her career on Broadway as a theatrical production assistant, Suzanne always believed she was destined for more. After technical difficulties on the set of *Sweet Charity* with Christina Applegate required the cast to repeat the musical number "*There's gotta be something better than this*" 23 times, the message to reinvent her life was received loud and clear. Exploring various options, she discovered the TV series *Starting Over* and immediately hired a life coach to help navigate her uncharted path.

Connecting with the notion of helping others, she started her own coaching practice, but her consistent advice of "get over yourself and move on" wasn't exactly conducive to effective personal development. During this time, however, she discovered her innate talent for teaching entrepreneurs how to create fast-growing, highly profitable endeavors and has quickly gained notoriety as one of the best business coaches in the industry.

Suzanne is a **Reinventor** and her *WHAT* is defined below. Visit SuzanneEvans.org for more information.

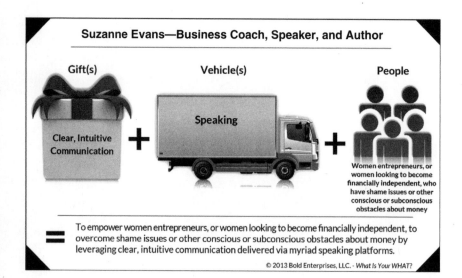

Suzanne Evans—Business Coach, Speaker, and Author

Gift(s)   Vehicle(s)   People

Clear, Intuitive Communication + Speaking + Women entrepreneurs, or women looking to become financially independent, who have shame issues or other conscious or subconscious obstacles about money

= To empower women entrepreneurs, or women looking to become financially independent, to overcome shame issues or other conscious or subconscious obstacles about money by leveraging clear, intuitive communication delivered via myriad speaking platforms.

© 2013 Bold Enterprises, LLC. - *What Is Your WHAT?*

You've Found Your WHAT...Now What?!

You were born to win. But to be a winner, you must plan to win, prepare to win, and expect to win.

—Hilary Hinton "Zig" Ziglar

Identifying your WHAT may bring you a sense of purpose more powerful than you could have ever imagined. Life without purpose is frightening, yet most people drift along directionless, going wherever the road happens to take them. Now that you've found your WHAT, your personal GPS resides at the forefront of your soul. It's there to call upon whenever you feel lost.

That said, it's unrealistic to instantly start a new career pursuing your WHAT. To bring your WHAT to fruition you'll need to:

- Identify your target market
- Nail your niche
- Create a winning game plan
- Begin a patient but steady transition

Your degree of fulfillment and success will largely depend on your ability to address each of these requirements. Let's take a closer look at how to identify your target market.

Find Those Who Are Waiting for You

Marketing success is a byproduct of micromarketing. No matter how tiny you believe your niche might be, there's probably sufficient demand to establish a thriving enterprise. Did you know that there are more than 100,000 people who identify themselves as left-handed quilters? Or that there are vendors who sell wigs for cats and dogs? Or that a decade-old sandwich that appeared to contain the image of the Virgin Mary sold for $28,000? Whoever your target audience is, they're ready and waiting for you to add value to their lives.

That said, connecting with your potential customers at precisely the right time they're interested in your message is highly challenging. While the "If you build it, they will come" approach worked for Kevin Costner's character in *Field of Dreams*, it seldom does in real life.

To create a sustainable business, you need to fully understand who your audience is, how they define themselves, what they need, how to reach them, and how to most effectively communicate with and persuade them to purchase your products and/or services. You can accomplish this using a variety of research tools, ranging from Google and social media to surveys and the tools available at your local library.

The more information you have, the easier it'll be to practice precision targeting (vs. a shotgun approach). This will save you time and money, maximizing your return on investment.

The following are key demographic details about your target market you'll eventually need to pinpoint. Fill in what you know now, and complete the rest as you learn more over time:

Gender: _____

Age range: _____

Religion: _____

Marital status: _____

Number of children: _____

Level of education: _____

Political views: _____

Ethnicity: _____

Occupation: _____

City they live in: _____

State they live in: _____

Country they live in: _____

Suburban/Urban/Rural: _____

Language(s) they speak: _____

Annual income: _____

What they read: _____

Websites they visit: _____

Mobile apps they use: _____

Sports they watch: _____

Hobbies: _____

Email newsletters they subscribe to: _____

Who they admire: _____

Music/Artists they like: _____

Television shows they watch: _____

Where they travel to: _____

Associations they belong to: _____

Events/conferences they attend: _____

Where they volunteer: _____

Where they shop: _____

Car they drive: _____

Rent or own their house/apartment: _____

Pets: _____

Other: _____

Fully completing your target market profile will take time and effort, but it'll put you miles ahead in the game. Few marketers invest in collecting such data and that's largely why most businesses fail.

Another important component of your profile is identifying your audience's frustrations, worries, and needs. Once you truly understand your market, you'll be in a position to convert prospects into lifelong customers. Do your best to fill in the following (modifying details as needed):

1. Patrick is the ideal beneficiary of my products and services. He is _____ years old and lives in _____.

2. He is deathly afraid that _____.

3. Often, he wakes up at 2 a.m. concerned about _____
    _____.

4. If I could help him _____,
    _____, and _____
    _____, I would have
    a customer for life.

5. If he could wake up tomorrow with the following three issues solved, his
    life would change dramatically for the better:

    a. _____

    b. _____

    c. _____

6. At some point in life, he experienced _____
    _____. Because of this, he is
    receptive to my message.

7. The single biggest obstacle to him purchasing my products and services is
    _____.

8. That said, he may have already purchased products from _____,
    _____, and _____ to help
    him address his concerns.

9. Because of this, he is skeptical that _____
    _____.

10. The solution he most needs is _____
    _____.

11. To help him gain comfort in taking advantage of my products' offer-
    ings, I will need to _____ and
    _____.

12. The search words and phrases he's most likely to use when surfing the
    Internet are _____,
    _____ and, _____.

13. To assist him in attaining his desired goals and objectives, or over-
    come his biggest obstacles, I will provide him with _____
    _____, _____
    _____, and,
    _____.

14. It's likely that if I can help him solve his problems, help him get from point A
    to point B, or help him take his life or business to the next level, he would pay
    _____ for my offerings. This is a fraction of its
    worth because, to him, _____
    is priceless.

Don't be concerned about how much or little you're able to answer right now. This exercise is designed to open your mind to the possibilities of nailing your audience profile and shifting from shooting bats in the dark to catching fish in a barrel.

Data, information, and demographic details are your most valuable weapons in your marketing arsenal. An effective marketer has the answers *before* writing copy, placing ads, and seeking customers.

Too many business owners are ready to write checks long before they're ready to cash them. Don't make that mistake.

Creating a Postcard for Your Business

A good way to think more clearly about your business is to fit it onto a postcard. Because the space is so limited, this forces you to identify clearly and concisely the essence of what you're offering to your target market.

For example, imagine a one-sentence headline in the top left-hand corner of the front of a postcard that immediately captures the interest of your prospects by addressing their single biggest need. Also consider the demographic details that represent to whom your postcard will be sent. Figure 17.1 shows an example.

Now create your own front side of a postcard using the template shown in Figure 17.2

Next, we'll flip over to the back of the postcard. It should contain a killer headline, important details that spark interest to learn more, and a shroud of mystery that requires action in order to receive an answer. It's a delicate balance that few execute well. That's why the world's best copywriters earn extraordinary fees as masters of their craft.

Let's break down the core components of an effective marketing message.

Headline

Your headline is the single most important component of your marketing campaign. An effective headline should serve as both the hook to cultivate interest and as incentive for the reader to take immediate action. Consider the following headline from Susan G. Komen for The Cure, which captures immediate interest and also spurs the reader to take immediate action:

Help cure breast cancer and save women's lives.

For the dual audiences of women with breast cancer and those who want to help women with breast cancer, this is a brilliant headline. It's clear, concise, and to the point. Best of all, it includes an implied call to action—when you read it, you're subtly made to feel that if you *don't* take action you don't really care about curing breast cancer or saving women's lives. The result is a high response rate.

```
┌─────────────────────────────────────────────────────────────────┐
│ ┌───────────────────┐                              ┌───────────┐ │
│ │                   │                              │   Stamp   │ │
│ │ You Were Born to Do│                             │           │ │
│ │ One Amazing Thing.│                              │           │ │
│ │ Discover It Now... for│                          │           │ │
│ │      FREE!        │                              └───────────┘ │
│ │                   │  ┌──────────────────────────────────────┐  │
│ └───────────────────┘  │ NAME: English-Speaking Female 44–59 Years Old │
│                        │                                      │  │
│                        │ ADDRESS: Single Family Home          │  │
│                        │                                      │  │
│                        │ CITY: Middle to High-Income Community│  │
│                        │                                      │  │
│                        │ STATE: Democratic State              │  │
│                        │                                      │  │
│                        │ ZIP CODE: Democratic Zip Code        │  │
│                        │                                      │  │
│                        │ COUNTRY: United States, UK, Canada, or Australia │
│                        └──────────────────────────────────────┘  │
└─────────────────────────────────────────────────────────────────┘
```

Figure 17.1   Sample Completed Postcard Front

```
┌─────────────────────────────────────────────────────────────────┐
│ ┌───────────────────┐                              ┌───────────┐ │
│ │ Headline:         │                              │   Stamp   │ │
│ │                   │                              │           │ │
│ │                   │                              │           │ │
│ │                   │                              └───────────┘ │
│ │                   │  ┌──────────────────────────────────────┐  │
│ │                   │  │ NAME: _____ │  │
│ │                   │  │ ADDRESS: _____ │  │
│ └───────────────────┘  │ CITY:      _____ │  │
│                        │ STATE: _____                     │  │
│                        │ ZIP CODE: _____           │  │
│                        │ COUNTRY: _____ │  │
│                        └──────────────────────────────────────┘  │
└─────────────────────────────────────────────────────────────────┘
```

Figure 17.2   Template for Your Postcard Front

In its ad for QuietComfort 15 Acoustic Noise Cancelling headphones, Bose uses this headline:

> *You'll love what you hear . . . and what you don't.*

In just nine words, the headline makes clear it's targeting audiophiles who want to "hear music in all of its glory without the distraction of background noise" and "perhaps even discover new depths and subtleties." These headphones aren't for everyone; the ad later offers "12 easy payments," so the price for such extraordinary technology is high. On the up side, this creates a cache for its owners. This well-crafted headline matches its target audience's internal dialogue.

Think about what an effective headline might be for your marketing message and write it on the lines that follow:

_____

_____

Body

Your body text reinforces your headline and also provides additional details relevant to your audience's needs. Put another way, the headline (or hook) captures attention and the body maintains it.

In the Susan G. Komen ad, the body describes three women, Alantheia, Sonia, and Marian, who "received support that helped each woman afford her screenings and surgeries." The ad then introduces Bridget, who Komen "helped find a doctor who actually believes she has a fighting chance." This language is powerful and moves the reader towards taking action.

The Bose ad establishes its competitive advantage by stating that "no other headphones offer you the same combination of less noise, lifelike music, lasting quality, and a comfortable fit." It also provides social proof via an endorsement from one of its customers, Murray Hill of Canada.com, who says, "These are fabulous."

Of all the elements for enhancing the body of your message, social proof may be the most powerful. When existing customers come forward to highly recommend you, your audience tends to feel a lot more comfortable about opening their wallets to make a positive purchase decision.

Create the body of your postcard, including social proof, and write it in the space that follows:

_____

_____

_____

_____

_____

_____

_____

_____

Call to Action

No effective marketing message is complete without the inclusion of a specific *call to action*, which instructs customers on how to take the next step. Whether it's "To order or learn more: 1-800-xxx or visit Bose.com/America," "Visit komen.org," or "Receive a free brochure and a $500 discount off your next purchase by . . . ," the goal is to transform the audience from neutral observer to active participant.

The degree to which a potential customer becomes actively involved with your marketing is known as his *engagement level*. The greater the engagement, the more likely it is he'll turn into a paying customer. Your marketing should therefore provide strong incentives for taking action. Effective call-to-action strategies include:

- Coupons ("$200 off for mentioning this ad")
- Risk-free trials ("Try it for free for 30 days. Don't like it? Send it back, no questions asked.")
- Interest-free financing ("12 easy payments with no interest charges")
- Bonuses ("Buy one and we'll send you another one free if you order by this date.")
- Time-sensitive offers ("This offer expires March 30th.")
- Third-party benefits ("Earn 1,200 AA Advantage miles from Bose when you order.")
- Related products and services ("Receive a free 30-minute phone consultation with one of our licensed tech gurus with your order.")
- Freebies ("Visit www.InternetProphets.com/free to download your free copy now!")

Figure 17.3   Scan the QR Code For Your Free Copy of *Internet Prophets*

Your call-to-action should also include a tracking code (e.g., a unique URL such as www.TheReinventionWorkshop.com/postcard) so you can monitor the effectiveness of your marketing efforts.

Think about what your call-to-action might be and write it below:

_____

_____

A completed back of a postcard might look like Figure 17.4.

Complete your own back of the postcard using the template discussed. The Headline goes first, followed by the Body, and then the Call to Action.

Once you've identified your target market and created your audience profile, there are numerous free and low-cost tools you can use to reach your customers. Many answers to the question "How do I share my Gifts with the world without going broke?" can be found in my award-winning book, *Internet Prophets: The World's Leading Experts Reveal How to Profit Online*. Grab your free copy of the entire book at www.InternetProphets.com/free or by scanning the QR code (Figure 17.3).

I am only one, but still I am one. I cannot do everything, but still I can do something. And because I cannot do everything, I will not refuse to do the something that I can do.

—Edward Everett Hale (historian and Unitarian clergyman, 1902)

Are you in a job you don't like? Are you unemployed? Are you in a state of transition and want to identify what's next? Do you believe that you were born to do something extraordinary, but just can't figure out what it is?

Then I have some really good news for you—*The Reinvention Workshop* will forever change your life. And because you've received this postcard, you can the take first powerful step towards becoming who you were born to be right now... for FREE!

"Steve Olsher's *Reinvention Workshop* is uplifting, inspiring, and filled with great ideas for people who are struggling with a next move in their careers or in personal transitions."
                                                                                      –Karen Ide

Receive FREE access to The Reinvention Workshop before March 1.
Visit TheReinventionWorkshop.com/postcard now for details.
The world is waiting for you!

Figure 17.4   Sample Completed Postcard Back

Nail Your Niche

Avoid working in commodity-driven markets where price is king, and service and originality means almost nothing, as this will inevitably lead to frustration.

George Washington Carver said, "When you can do the common things in life in an uncommon way, you will command the attention of the world." To become one-of-a-kind as opposed to one-of-many, create your own market, establish yourself as the only choice within your defined area of expertise, charge a premium for your services—and have the world knocking down your door to benefit from your unique talents.

By identifying your *WHAT*, you've taken the first step towards achieving greatness, but you must also decide how to use your Gift in a focused way. Let's look at three examples that illustrate the importance of focus.

Café Du Monde's Beignets

Café Du Monde in New Orleans is known for one item—beignets. A beignet (which is French for "doughnut") is a square piece of fried dough covered in powdered sugar. One order consists of three pieces and costs $2.36. Established in 1862 in New Orleans' French Market, Café Du Monde is open 24 hours a day, 7 days a week (with the exception of Christmas and the occasional hurricane). Its entire menu consists of beignets, dark roasted coffee and chicory, white and chocolate milk, fresh-squeezed orange juice, and soft drinks. By focusing on one ordinary thing—essentially a fancy doughnut—and producing it in an extraordinary manner, this vendor has achieved remarkable success.

Allstar Electrical Services

Allstar Electrical Services in Denver, Colorado, has been in business since 2000 and earned an A rating on *Angie's List*. Allstar concentrates on residential and commercial work, with a focus on repairs and remodeling.

"We're experts in electrical installation for residential and commercial jobs, both indoors and outdoors, and focus on remodeling and repairs," says owner Gary Stone. "We don't do framing, drywall, plumbing, heating, roofing or windows. We do electrical work, and we do it better than anyone." While there's a natural urge to expand offerings to take on a broader scope of work, Stone resists such temptation by concentrating on what he does best—electrical work—and continues to grow his business as a result.

Sean Rich of Tortuga Trading

Sean Rich is the President and CEO of Tortuga Trading in Carlsbad, California. The company specializes in antique arms and armament from all over the world, concentrating on the sixteenth through nineteenth centuries. Sean's love for the past began at age 10 when he acquired his first antique weapon. Over the years, he's participated in numerous archaeological digs. He was designated New Jersey's state representative for Gulf Coast Rare Coins and Investments, specializing in treasure recovered from the Spanish Galleon Atocha and 1715 Plate Fleet.

Sean's expertise led to a three-year stint as a weapons consultant for Walt Disney Studios' Second Mate Productions, covering the second and third *Pirates of the Caribbean* movies. In 2009, Sean began working as an antique arms and armament specialist for Leftfield Pictures, the production company of numerous series including The History Channel's *Pawn Stars*. Whenever rare arms or armament from the sixteenth through nineteenth centuries show up at the pawnshop, the owners automatically call Sean. By becoming an expert in a specific field, Sean has created his own market, is able to charge a premium for it, and has the world knocking down his door to pay for what comes most naturally to him . . . his WHAT.

This is your goal. Do one thing, do it better than anyone else, and get paid extraordinarily well for your talent.

Think about the most successful people you know—the lawyer who takes on only fathers' rights cases, the dentist who specializes in pediatric root canals, the teacher who focuses on troubled teens. They've all become experts in one specific arena, dedicated their lives to it, and are compensated at levels far superior to those of their counterparts.

Getting to this point, however, is a journey.

It took me years to recognize that while business and personal development are my fields of interest, my WHAT is helping people NICHETIZE!—that is, identify their WHAT and teach them how to monetize it.

Many doctors begin as general practitioners before deciding on their specialty. The majority of successful entrepreneurs endured multiple business failures before creating ventures that make the most of their passion. You will undergo a similar process.

To pursue the WHAT you've identified, take the next steps: create a winning game plan, and begin a patient but steady transition.

The Game Plan

John Wooden is the greatest college basketball coach in history. As head coach of the UCLA Bruins from 1948 to 1975, Wooden led the Bruins to an unprecedented 10 NCAA titles, four perfect 30-0 seasons, and a record winning streak of 88 games. Wooden attributes much of his success to his unwavering mantra:

"Failure to prepare is preparing to fail."

As UCLA amassed victory after victory, Coach Wooden refused to rest on his laurels. He prepared a detailed game plan for each opponent while visualizing his intended outcome. Every season, Coach Wooden's ultimate objective was to win the national championship. This required his team to be victorious as often as possible during the regular season and to win each tournament game. It also meant that each individual player had to outperform his counterpart.

His players understood this. They recognized that the result of *each play* had meaningful impact on whether or not UCLA would win the NCAA Championship. In other words, they all stayed focused on their ultimate objective and took steps on a day-by-day and moment-by-moment basis to achieve it.

You should adopt a similar strategy in pursuit of your *WHAT*. In order to reach the top of the mountain, there are three critical steps you'll need to take.

Identify Your Ultimate Objective

Steve Jobs said, "We're here to put a dent in the universe." Be clear on your objective and maintain laser-like focus on making it happen.

Imagine what living your *WHAT* will look and feel like. The more vividly you can create a mental scene of your goal, the more likely you are to realize it.

Add details to the scene by asking yourself such questions as:

- What city am I living in?
- Do I travel? If so, how often?
- Do I work solo from home or in a large office with hundreds of colleagues?
- Do I have employees who report to me? If so, how many?
- How much money do I make?
- Am I famous?
- How large is my audience?
- Who are my clients?
- What extraordinary things am I going to do with my *WHAT*?

Think about what's most important to you and write down your Ultimate Objective in the space that follows:

_____

_____

_____

_____

_____

Identify the Steps That Lead to Your Ultimate Objective

Pursuing your *WHAT* may seem like an overwhelming task. Breaking the process down into small steps you can readily envision will make it feel more concrete and achievable.

For example, after discovering her *WHAT*, a participant in The Reinvention Workshop identified her Ultimate Objective as teaching a spirituality writing class. We defined the steps required to reach that goal:

1. Establish her niche and hook—that is, her unique offering.
2. Take classes, research what others are doing, intern, and imitate those she admires.
3. Write the first sentence of her book and/or classroom materials.
4. Enlist trusted sources to review her plan, and provide feedback and support (monetary or emotional).
5. Create her classroom materials and website.
6. Clarify details about her audience (e.g., who will attend, ideal number of participants, costs).
7. Secure the venue.
8. Rehearse her presentation.
9. Identify her target audience and market the class via her website, social media, fliers, PR, networking, advertising, and sponsors.
10. Register participants.
11. Prepare the venue.
12. Begin the class.

Can you develop a comprehensive plan that will remain effective in every aspect years from now? Of course not, because the other side of the coin is John Lennon's famous observation:

> *"Life is what happens to you while you're busy making other plans."*

Just because life is unpredictable doesn't mean you shouldn't have plans, though. It simply means that you should be flexible and adaptable, and always ready to change in response to the unexpected.

With this in mind, I want you to identify the steps that lead to your Ultimate Objective. Your final goal, naturally, is to reach it. So write your Ultimate Objective on the first line and work backwards to identify the first step, which should be something you can begin doing today.

Many find that working backwards is easier than starting with the present. If you prefer to start with today and work forward, that's fine too.

Then again, if this process is making little sense and you feel too overwhelmed to start, put down this book and embrace all the ways the world is eager to help. Buy books on your subject matter, take classes, hire a coach, intern, join a free group, and/or apprentice yourself to a mentor.

And use the Internet. It offers information on almost anything you can think of—there are even free online videos on how to break into most major professions. Someone who's already living out your *WHAT* is probably writing a free blog and selling a newsletter, book, or DVD full of helpful information.

In other words, you don't have to start completely from scratch. Find people who are doing what you want to do and shadow them until you figure out their process.

Once you're ready to identify the steps required to reach your Ultimate Objective, please write them on the lines that follow. While this will be just a first draft, it'll inspire you to reach your Ultimate Objective by breaking the process down into manageable pieces.

ULTIMATE OBJECTIVE: _____

STEP 12: _____

STEP 11: _____

STEP 10: _____

STEP 9: _____

STEP 8: _____

STEP 7: _____

STEP 6: _____

STEP 5: _____

STEP 4: _____

STEP 3: _____

STEP 2: _____

STEP 1 (TODAY): _____

Becoming who you were born to be requires a great deal of effort. Having some sense of the path you'll be traveling will help you prepare for whatever you might face along the way. By defining the steps required to reach your Ultimate Objective, you substantially increase the odds of it happening.

Begin

This may sound easy enough, but I can't overemphasize its importance. All the planning in the world is worthless until you start acting on those plans.

Your first small step towards achieving your Ultimate Objective is actually a monumental leap forward . . . because you've now entered The Transition.

The Transition

While finding your WHAT and creating your game plan are crucial turning points, you won't magically turn into a master of your chosen field. The transition to living your WHAT takes time. It's within this period of advancing from where you are now to where you want to be that you'll make yourself humble and vulnerable, take risks, learn your trade, hone your skills, and solidify your understanding of what it means to live out your WHAT on a daily basis.

Your transition will be a work in progress. It's not unusual to modify a life plan several times as you move from your mental destination to reality. Be patient as you learn and develop your skills.

Meanwhile, don't quit your day job or kill a cash-producing cow. If you were a real estate developer in your former career and own a three-flat that generates monthly income, keep it. Simply because you're on a new quest doesn't require you to take drastic measures. Earn while you learn. Then gradually begin shifting your schedule to invest more and more time on your WHAT.

While working towards your WHAT, you may be pleasantly surprised at how issues that once bothered you lose much of their impact.

I think of the transition as an evolving recipe. Today your recipe is 100 parts current vocation and 0 parts WHAT. After you earn your first dollar from your WHAT, your recipe shifts to 99.9 parts current vocation and .1 parts WHAT.

If you stay focused on your Ultimate Objective, at some point you'll reach 70 parts WHAT and 30 parts current vocation, or 80 parts WHAT and 20 parts current vocation. You'll know when it's time to cut the rope.

Nothing worthwhile comes without its challenges. You may need to intern, take on whatever jobs you can to pay the bills, and sacrifice to get there. But as pointed out by nationally syndicated radio host Dave Ramsey in his book *The Total Money Makeover*, "If you will live like no one else, later you can live like no one else."

Meanwhile, stay focused on your game plan, talk to everyone you know about it, latch onto a mentor (or two), and maintain a positive frame of mind. You'll soon be like a Moto Guzzi on a straightaway . . . nothing will slow you down unless you apply the brakes.

Fulfilling your WHAT as your full-time vocation is now in sight. Commit to making it happen, and in time it will.

A Final Thought About Your WHAT

Every year *Parade* magazine runs a cover story titled "What People Earn" that shows a broad range of people in different professions and their annual salaries. It's a well-done snapshot of American employment—and its information is shocking.

A farmhand in Iowa might make $25,000 a year. Meanwhile, a professional tennis player could be pulling down $35 million. What's especially intriguing is that the people earning the most money are those about whom others might say, "They're not working very hard."

Famous actors, great athletes, acclaimed CEOs, and other stars actually put in a tremendous number of hours to master their professions. But to those who break their backs to make $25,000 a year, those at the top often appear to be having a picnic in the park while getting paid a fortune to do so.

That's actually the beauty of achieving your WHAT. Work should be fun, and you should be paid extraordinarily well for it.

Your goal is for your work to directly reflect who you inherently are. When this happens, what you may perceive as an avocation will become your vocation, and your life will become a vacation.

Are you ready?

You've Found Your WHAT . . . Now What?!—Takeaways

- You deserve to reap extraordinary financial rewards for doing what you were born to do.
- To achieve your *WHAT*:
  - Identify your target market.
  - Nail your niche.
  - Create a winning game plan.
  - Begin a patient but steady transition.
- As John Wooden said, "Failure to prepare is preparing to fail."
- As Steve Jobs said, "We're here to put a dent in the universe."
- As John Lennon said, "Life is what happens to you while you're busy making other plans."
- Identify your Ultimate Objective, define the steps that lead to your Ultimate Objective . . . and begin.
- Someone has already forged the path for you—follow it.
- Discuss your game plan with others.
- Turn what you may perceive as an avocation into your vocation—and get ready for life to become a vacation.

WHAT IS YOUR *WHAT?*
Case Study #17: Jonny Imerman

Jonny Imerman is the founder and executive director of Imerman Angels, a non-profit that matches anyone seeking cancer support with a "mentor angel"—that is, a cancer survivor who is the same age, gender, and most importantly, has beaten the same type of cancer. The service is absolutely free and helps anyone touched by any type of cancer, at any cancer stage level, at any age, living anywhere in the world.

Jonny began his career in commercial real estate after graduating from the University of Michigan. At 26, while pursuing his M.B.A., he was diagnosed with testicular cancer and began his fight against the disease. Throughout his experience, he was fortunate to have loving support from family and friends, but had never met, nor had access to, someone his age that survived cancer and truly understood his plight. After the removal of his left testicle, extensive chemotherapy, the reappearance and removal of four malignant tumors from his spine, and a two-and-a-half year battle, he was finally cancer free.

Vowing to help others avoid the fate of having to battle cancer alone, he began connecting people afflicted with the disease to survivors who can lend support and empathy as well as direction for navigating the system, determining their options, and creating their own support systems. Today, Imerman Angels has eight full-time employees and matches thousands globally every year.

Jonny is a *Reinventor* and his *WHAT* is defined below. Visit ImermanAngels.org for more information.

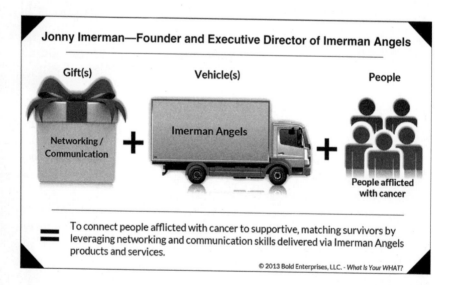

Jonny Imerman—Founder and Executive Director of Imerman Angels

Gift(s)   Vehicle(s)   People

Networking / Communication

Imerman Angels

People afflicted with cancer

= To connect people afflicted with cancer to supportive, matching survivors by leveraging networking and communication skills delivered via Imerman Angels products and services.

© 2013 Bold Enterprises, LLC. - *What Is Your WHAT?*

Forge Your Path,
Create Your Legacy

As a single footstep will not make a path on the Earth, so a single thought will not make a pathway in the mind. To make a deep physical path, we walk again and again. To make a deep mental path, we must think over and over the kind of thoughts we wish to dominate our lives.

—Henry David Thoreau

If you've patiently worked your way through the previous chapters, I hope you've experienced an incredible journey. You should now have a profoundly better understanding of who you are and what to do with your life.

That said, there's one more exercise to tackle—writing your *Letter of Reflection*. Your letter will provide a concise summation of the goals you've identified and help keep you on point as you share your Gifts with the world.

My personal reinvention began after having a vision of my funeral. The words being spoken graveside ring as loudly now as they did then: "Here lies Steve Olsher. He devoted his life to chasing the almighty dollar."

I suddenly realized that aside from family and friends, the only one who substantially benefited from my existence was me, me, and—did I mention—me. I began to think about how to best use the years I had left and started wondering what accomplishments I could look back on towards the end of my life that would make me feel proud.

Interestingly, none of them involved making money.

While I'd enjoyed moderate success as an entrepreneur, it became clear that everything I'd done as a professional was focused on profit. I'd like to think that my real estate developments provide comfortable places for people to live and work, but if I were to die tomorrow, my tenants wouldn't be lining up to pay their final respects; they'd simply want to know where to send their rent check.

Liquor.com is an awesome website if you're looking for an expert guide to cocktails and spirits, but there are tens of thousands of online resources that offer niche-focused information.

My aim is to have a more meaningful impact on the world.

Writing this book, creating and facilitating The Reinvention Workshop, and, I hope, helping you find your destiny is my way of heeding that call. What I now realize is there's a significant difference between living well and living for the sake of making money.

Don't get me wrong; each of us is entitled to make a great living. I'm not one of those people who would suggest you resign yourself to life as a starving artist simply because you're compelled to draw.

What I *am* saying is that we're all obligated by our common bond of humanity to not only pursue what brings us financial success, but what also makes a positive impact on our community, our environment, and our world.

With this in mind, in 2009 I wrote my Letter of Reflection. My goal was to envision a life I'd be proud to remember in my final days.

Completing my Letter of Reflection revitalized my sense of purpose. It concisely sums up what I want to accomplish between the day I wrote it and the day I leave this world.

Writing your own Letter of Reflection is a highly effective way to face your mortality, realize your time on this planet is limited, and provide you with direction and motivation to achieve the goals dearest to you.

As Stephen Covey wrote in *The 7 Habits of Highly Effective People*, "You must begin with the end in mind." Not to be morbid, but nothing represents "the end" more than death.

Take a few quiet moments to imagine yourself in your final days. Now ask yourself these questions:

- How do I feel about the life I lived?
- Am I happy about how my life affected the world?

- Did my life have the meaning I intended?
- Did I accomplish the things most important to me?
- When I imagine the people visiting me in my final days, do I sense they feel real loss, or are they there simply because they feel obligated?

Chances are, most of your answers may not be positive. The good news is, you're still alive. And while tomorrow isn't a given, you can immediately begin constructing the life and legacy you desire and take full advantage of however many years are left to you.

First, try to identify all the things you most want to accomplish. Look through your answers to this book's exercises, and deep within, for inspiration. Now answer these questions:

1. What and/or who is most important to you?

   _____

2. Do you have a personal mantra? If so, what is it?

   _____

3. What is your life's purpose?

   _____

4. How do you want to be remembered by those who knew you best?

   _____

5. How do you want to be remembered by those who knew you only by name?

   _____

6. What are you committed to accomplishing before you die?

   _____

7. What principles, processes, and/or skills are you committed to mastering?

   _____

8. How did you define your WHAT?

   _____

9. In one sentence, to what will you dedicate your life from this point forward?

   _____

To become who you were born to be, it's essential to create goals and objectives that serve to both anchor you from diversions and steer you toward your destiny.

Your Letter of Reflection represents the culmination of your journey with this book. You've mastered The Four Stages of Learning, The Vortex of Vulnerability, The Vortex of Invincibility, and The Pinnacle. You've lived The Seven Life-Altering Principles and discovered your WHAT.

With these in mind, write your Letter of Reflection in the space that follows. Begin with the end in mind. Everything else will fall into place.

_____
_____
_____
_____
_____
_____
_____
_____
_____
_____

If you've completed your *Letter of Reflection*, I hope it proved illuminating to create. Refer to it whenever you feel adrift; it will serve as a powerful guide to your future.

Consider what you've written a first draft. It's a good idea to revise your Letter of Reflection periodically—once a year or so—to reflect changes in your life. If you keep each draft, you'll end up with a fascinating record of your process of transformation, and how your hopes and dreams evolved over time.

The Beginning of Your Journey

You've reached the end of this book's exercises but merely the beginning of your journey. The world awaits the Gifts you have to share.

As nineteenth century attorney and Civil War officer Henry Hancock wisely observed,

Out of our beliefs are born deeds;

Out of our deeds we form habits;

Out of our habits grows our character;

And on our character we build our destiny.

Living life in a powerful manner requires that you choose to live powerfully. Pursue living as who you were born to be and you'll achieve your true destiny.

A Final Word

In 1859, politician and education advocate Horace Mann advised, "Be ashamed to die until you have won some victory for mankind." How are you going to leave your mark? What will your contribution be?

You have the capacity to make an extraordinary difference in the lives of those around you, as well as benefit generations to come.

While you transition towards becoming who you were born to be, remember that those who have made their mark—people such as Richard Branson, Sam Zell, Sean Combs, and Mother Teresa—all began just like you. None were born with silver spoons in their mouths. Their journey began by taking a first step. They then consistently chose paths most congruent with who they inherently are.

Virgin founder Richard Branson started by selling one record at a time through a mail-order business. Real estate and media tycoon Sam Zell convinced one landlord to let him manage his building. Entertainment mogul Sean Combs interned at Uptown Records before becoming an executive and eventually, releasing his first album. Mother Teresa sought to bring comfort to one person in need.

Each experienced hardship. Each experienced failure. Each persevered. To attain meaningful satisfaction and contentment, heed the words of Buddha: "It is better to travel well than to arrive." This is an essential mind-set for cultivating ultimate achievement.

Remember, the destination is the road. The journey is the destination.

Savor each step along your new path.

The End of Our Journey Together

Enormous congratulations for completing *What Is Your WHAT?* Discovering who you were born to be and, hopefully, beginning the process of personal reinvention are incredible accomplishments.

This journey has required you to explore the very depths of your being. You may have experienced some discomfort, and even pain, along the way as you shed self-destructive habits. I applaud you for sticking with it. By completing this book and pursuing what you've learned, I'm confident you'll enjoy profound and long-lasting, positive change.

I'd love to hear about how *What Is Your WHAT?* affected you. Please email me at Steve@SteveOlsher.com.

Please also feel encouraged to join the *What Is Your WHAT?* community and receive my monthly *NICHETIZE!* newsletter at WhatIsYourWhat.com. As a special bonus for signing up, you'll receive exclusive access to over 20 hours of video footage from the interviews I conducted with those who shared their *WHAT* at the end of each chapter. Gain invaluable insight as to how Larry Winget, Marci Shimoff, Dan Miller, Guy Kawasaki, Mari Smith, and others traversed their respective minefields to discover what they are truly compelled to do.

If you're interested in working together, I encourage you to apply to join my private year-long coaching program, The Circle of 10. Over the course of 12 months, I'll help you identify your WHAT, create a powerful plan of action for bringing your WHAT to fruition, and teach you how to monetize what you're compelled to do. Enrollment is limited to just 60 hand-selected people from across the globe per year. Nothing will build your business faster or empower you to share your Gifts with the world in a more expedited fashion than working with me personally. More information can be found at CircleOf10.com.

If you'd like to learn more about The Reinvention Workshop, how you can become a certified Reinvention Workshop teacher and assist people in discovering their WHAT, or take the Workshop either online or in person, please visit TheReinventionWorkshop.com.

To access free NICHETIZE! training, content-laden webinars, or for our schedule of upcoming events, please visit SteveOlsher.com.

Lastly, to book me as a speaker, media guest, or to just drop me a line and say "hello," please contact me at Steve@SteveOlsher.com.

I look forward to hearing from you.

In Closing

Consider the words of motivational speaker Les Brown:

"Most people fail in life not because they aim too high and miss, but because they aim too low and hit."

And some people never aim at all. I encourage you to aim as high as you can imagine . . . and then aim higher. Commandeer life by living like a sniper. Don't just endeavor to hit the target—aim for the center of the bull's eye.

The world is waiting for you!

Forge Your Path, Create Your Legacy—Takeaways

- There's a significant difference between living well and living for the sake of making money.
- We're all obligated by our common bond of humanity to pursue things that have a positive impact on our community, our environment, and our world.
- Your *Letter of Reflection* provides a sense of purpose and helps define what you hope to accomplish between now and the end of your life.
- As Stephen R. Covey wrote, "You must begin with the end in mind."
- Pursue living as who you were born to be and you'll achieve your true destiny.
- As Horace Mann said, "We should be ashamed to die until we have made some major contribution to mankind."
- To cultivate ultimate achievement, remember the words of Buddha: "It is better to travel well than to arrive."
- Living life in a powerful manner requires that you choose to live powerfully.
- The world is waiting for you!

WHAT IS YOUR *WHAT*?
Case Study #18: David Allen

David Allen is a consultant, speaker, and author of three best-selling books including *Getting Things Done: The Art of Stress-Free Productivity* which *Time* magazine called "the self-help business book of its time." His methodology for helping businesses and individuals effectively move planned tasks and projects out of the mind, record them externally, and break them down into actionable work items has become the benchmark productivity protocol for millions.

During his early career, David pursued various endeavors and worked in 35 industries before the age of 35. Fascinated by the relationship between the tangible and intangible, he leveraged his intuitive gifts and business experience to teach corporations how to handle pressing tasks with completion, elegance, and excellence. By implementing his strategies, clients unequivocally are able to clear space for new ideas to emerge and avoid distractions that prevent the organization from accomplishing its desired objectives.

A testament to one's willingness to persevere and attain certainty a project is completed correctly, David spent more than four years writing, rewriting, editing and, finally, releasing *Getting Things Done*. Its subsequent success has led to the creation of an exportable, translatable process that empowers others to teach the *Getting Things Done* system to thousands annually across the globe.

David is a *Reinventor* and his *WHAT* is defined below. Visit DavidCo.com for more information.

David Allen—Best-Selling Author, Consultant, and Speaker

Gift(s)

Clear, Relatable Communication

Vehicle(s)

Training, Speaking, and Writing

People

Those seeking to improve themselves and the world around them

To empower those seeking to improve themselves and the world around them to manifest their desired results by leveraging clear, relatable communication delivered via training, speaking, and writing.

© 2013 Bold Enterprises, LLC. - *What Is Your WHAT?*

ABOUT THE AUTHOR

S teve Olsher is America's Reinvention Expert. He's taught thousands how to NICHETIZE! (nitch-a-tize) by identifying and monetizing their WHAT—that is, the *one* thing they were born to do. His approach for achieving permanent, positive change blends his own proprietary methods with ancient wisdom and lessons from modern thought leaders, forming a proven system for ultimate achievement in business and in life.

Steve is the author of the 2012 Business Technology Book of the Year, *Internet Prophets: The World's Leading Experts Reveal How to Profit Online*; author of the 2010 Self-Help Book of the Year, *Journey To You: A Step-by-Step Guide to Becoming Who You Were Born to Be*; creator and host of *Internet Prophets LIVE!*; costar of the groundbreaking film *The Keeper of the Keys* with Jack Canfield, John Gray, and Marci Shimoff; and has appeared on ABC TV, NBC TV, FOX TV, CNBC.com, and more than 300 radio shows including national programs hosted by Lou Dobbs, Jim Bohannon, and Mancow Muller.

Steve is a successful entrepreneur who's applied his business acumen and communication skills to a wide range of endeavors. He's worked as a radio and nightclub DJ (Mr. Bold); owned his own alcohol-free nightclub at the age of 20 (The Funky Pickle!); launched the first wine and spirits store on CompuServe's Electronic Mall in 1993; launched one of the Internet's first ecommerce websites in 1995 (LiquorbyWire.com); started Bold Development, one of Chicago's largest boutique real estate development companies; is the cofounder and chairman of San Francisco-based Liquor.com; has earned the rank of brown belt in Brazilian Jiu-Jitsu training under the late Carlson Gracie Sr.; and is the creator and facilitator of The Reinvention Workshop.

All of Steve's varied experiences have contributed to the concepts found in his award-winning books.

Steve lives in Chicago with his wife Lena and their three sons, Bobby, Isaiah, and Xavier—who remind him every day why his motto is "Let Love Rule."

To learn more, and receive free *NICHETIZE!* training, please visit www .SteveOlsher.com.